To: Denny, friend an
wednesday night me
you enjoy some of th.
in rural Minnesota from long ago.
Jim Park

RUTHTON RECOLLECTIONS

by

JAMES W. PARK

MONTEZUMA PUBLISHING

Please direct comments regarding this product to:

Montezuma Publishing
Aztec Shops Ltd.
San Diego State University
San Diego, California 92182-1701
619-594-7552

or email: *montezuma@aztecmail.com*

website: www.montezumapublishing.com

Design and Layout: Kim A. Mazyck

Cover Art and Village of Ruthton Map by John V. Carter

John works as a designer in the field of residential architecture and currently resides in San Diego, CA

ISBN-10:   0-7442-3493-X
ISBN-13: 978-0-7442-3493-0

Preface

The notion of writing a few pages of recollections about grow-ing up in Ruthton, Minnesota in the 1940s and 1950s slowly came to me following the 2013 reunion of my class of 1954. Classes that graduated from 1951 to 1955 have organized joint reunions every five years beginning in the 1960s and continuing until the most recent one, that of 2013. Graduating classes averaged about fifteen to twenty-five students, so a joint reunion of all five classes was man-ageable, and each of us knew everyone from the other four classes. We have always had a large attendance, and the reunions have been spirited, nostalgia-filled celebrations of "the good old days." These "Recollections" stem from this compelling sense of nostalgia together with the feeling that those times in that place were spe-cial in our lives. In addition, I have always been curious about the growing-up experiences of my parents and grandparents in places such as Denmark, Iowa, South Dakota, and Minnesota. But the only thing my brother and I have from them is the oral history. This is an effort to offer a more lasting perspective. Finally, the repeated though irregular attendance at those class reunions which were usually held in Ruthton allowed me to observe changes in the town. Those changes also inspire this written recollection of the way it used to be.

My memories and those of friends and relatives form the basis for these recollections. They could have been formulated as a history, but because of the personal and informal nature of much of the material, *Ruthton Recollections* should not be treated as a history nor an autobiography. The stories and incidents chosen for inclusion were selected to illustrate the tenor of those times and the distinguishing characteristics of the period as I recall them. That selection process led to the omission of some stories whose inclusion could possibly have caused more pain than enlightenment for some readers. Finally, *Ruthton Centennial* (1988) provided a valuable source of detailed information used to verify these recollections and to supplement them.

In memory of my grandparents:

William C. Park and Clara Shaffer Park

Peter Christensen and Augusta Capion Christensen

My parents:

Floyd C. Park and Eva E. Park

Dedicated to my grandchildren:

James David (JD), Trevor, and Casey Park

Acknowledgements

In the first rank of those who offered support and encouragement for this project is the mother-daughter team, Cynthia D. Park and Hillary D. Park. Their enthusiasm for these recollections never flagged during the evolution of the manuscript. I am also deeply grateful to them for their candid stylistic and editorial suggestions. Without their strong interest in this undertaking, it would not have come to fruition. In addition, I am much indebted to the following family members, classsmates, and friends for their encouragement and their suggestions on editing and content. Their different perspectives and generous offers of information helped me avoid serious mistakes. The remaining errors are, of course, solely my responsibility. For this assistance I offer my earnest gratitude to: David Park, Donald Park, Kathy Park, Laura Park, Ken Anderson, Ethel Anderson, David Jackson, Harriet Anderson Olson, Russell Pilegaard, and Stephen Housley.

James W. Park, January 2017

Table of Contents

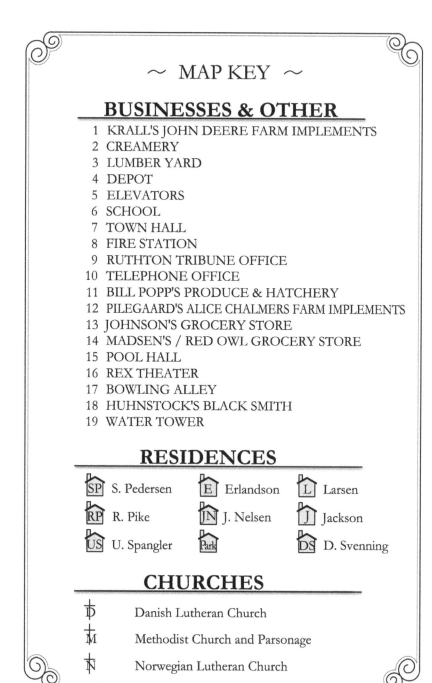

~ MAP KEY ~

BUSINESSES & OTHER

1 KRALL'S JOHN DEERE FARM IMPLEMENTS
2 CREAMERY
3 LUMBER YARD
4 DEPOT
5 ELEVATORS
6 SCHOOL
7 TOWN HALL
8 FIRE STATION
9 RUTHTON TRIBUNE OFFICE
10 TELEPHONE OFFICE
11 BILL POPP'S PRODUCE & HATCHERY
12 PILEGAARD'S ALICE CHALMERS FARM IMPLEMENTS
13 JOHNSON'S GROCERY STORE
14 MADSEN'S / RED OWL GROCERY STORE
15 POOL HALL
16 REX THEATER
17 BOWLING ALLEY
18 HUHNSTOCK'S BLACK SMITH
19 WATER TOWER

RESIDENCES

SP	S. Pedersen	E	Erlandson	L	Larsen
RP	R. Pike	JN	J. Nelsen	J	Jackson
US	U. Spangler	Park		DS	D. Svenning

CHURCHES

D̄   Danish Lutheran Church

M   Methodist Church and Parsonage

N̄   Norwegian Lutheran Church

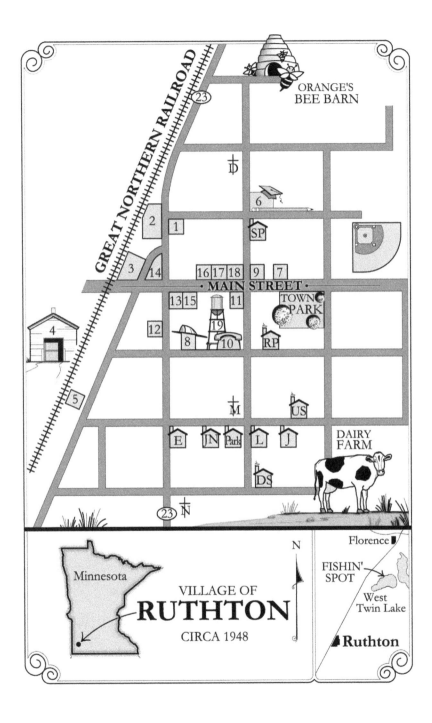

ORANGE'S
BEE BARN

GREAT NORTHERN RAILROAD

MAIN STREET

TOWN
PARK

DAIRY
FARM

N

Minnesota

VILLAGE OF
RUTHTON
CIRCA 1948

N

Florence

FISHIN'
SPOT

West
Twin Lake

Ruthton

9

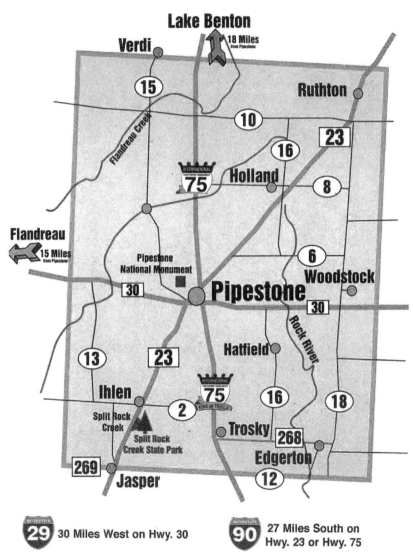

Pipestone County Map

James W. Park

Sunday Nights, Ruthton

When my grandparents would slowly come down the stairs about 5:30 pm carrying their contribution toward supper, it signaled the start of the traditional Sunday evening get-together of our family— parents, grandparents on my mother's side, and my brother Don, younger than I by three years. This supper consisted of homemade dinner rolls and varieties of cheese; lunch meat such as dried beef, summer sausage, and braunschweiger; potato salad, homemade pickles, and two or three varieties of homemade cookies. After a quick clean-up involving everyone except Dad and Grandpa, we all gathered around the large radio console in the living room for a couple of hours and listened to comedies such as "Amos 'n' Andy," "Jack Benny," and "The Edgar Bergen and Charlie McCarthy Show"; the comic quiz program "It Pays to Be Ignorant" and "The Kate Smith Hour" which always concluded with the popular singer's heartfelt rendition of "God Bless America." At some point in the evening we four "men" found time for a few hands of cards, usually smear or rummy. For a happy conclusion to the evening we shared a batch of fudge, fresh from the kitchen. Mom taught me how to make it when I was about 10 or 11, and thereafter the rule was simple: if you want

Park Family Photo

to enjoy fudge go ahead and make it. And I received encouragement from everyone. We always had the ingredients on hand, and I made sure to add a generous portion of walnuts to the mixture. This was not an extravagance because we often received a large burlap bag of walnuts for Christmas from Aunt Alice (Dad's sister) and Uncle Bill who lived in far distant Stockton, California. From a kid's perspective, the consumption of walnut-laden fudge was a great way to finish our family's Sunday night supper in our little town out on the prairie.

Ruthton, a small village in Minnesota where I grew up during the 1940s and 1950s, was founded in 1888 when a railroad was completed linking the area's agricultural hinterland to processing facilities in the Twin Cities. It is located in the state's southwestern corner in Pipestone County about 18 miles from the South Dakota border and 45 miles from Iowa. Cheap land attracted farmers during the next several decades, and they eventually settled the land at an initial density of about three or four families per section of land or 160 acres per farm. Most of the land was suitable for cultivation and grazing, and the main crops were corn, grain, and hay, and at the same time farmers usually raised some beef and dairy cattle, hogs, and poultry. Preferred crops changed somewhat over time in response to demand. Flax became a money crop in the late 1930s and especially in the war years; seeds were harvested and the straw was baled and used to produce cloth and high quality paper. A few farmers were known to have made enough from flax in one year to pay off the farm mortgage. One year in the early 1940s following a cool, damp spring in which the normal crops failed to germinate, Bertha Thompson reseeded her farm in flax and hit it big. Thereafter she received uncommon respect for her "uncanny astuteness!" In fact, it contributed to elevating her to the office of treasurer of the Methodist Ladies Aid. A crop that became widely cultivated in the 1950s was soybeans, and they have remained a popular crop to the present. Throughout those early decades farmers enjoyed a significant degree of self-sufficiency; they sold some surpluses locally but shipped quantities of corn, grain, and soybeans through the elevator by rail to the Twin Cities. Ruthton grew along with the rural population, serviced it, and became dependent on it.

By the early 1950s the town was approaching its best days. School consolidation represented a significant sign of progress at the start of the decade. It resulted in combining the several small, rural school districts in the surrounding area with Ruthton's elementary/secondary public school. Though seen at the time as a major step forward, it met some resistance, especially from those living in rural districts where the teacher was popular and well regarded. A few new homes were built following the certainty of consolidation. In fact, Clarence Jensen, owner of the Gamble Store and a prominent businessman, announced that he would build as soon as consolidation became a reality and he fulfilled his promise. Businesses also did well at that time. The hardships of the depression years and the forced frugality of the war years belonged to the past, and the agricultural economy was humming, thanks in part to "parity" or price supports for certain widely-cultivated farm commodities. Most residents enjoyed a modestly improving standard of living, and they could proclaim, "I like Ike," even if but quietly and only to their closest friends. After all, many of these same folks were part of the group that warmly welcomed President Harry Truman when his motorcade briefly paused in Ruthton while enroute to the Twin Cities during the election campaign of 1948.

The following census data from 1910 to 2010 for the town's population offers clear confirmation that the decade of the 1950s was Ruthton's heyday. It also suggests that the decline which began at some point in that same decade was continuous except for a pause in the 1980s after which it resumed its earlier downward path.

Ruthton Population, 1910-2010

1910	290	1970	405
1920	403	1980	328
1930	387	1990	328
1940	480	2000	284
1950	534	2010	241
1960	476		

Source: U.S. Census Reports

The decade after World War II was a great time to be entering adulthood. Ruthton boasted numbers of professionals and well-educated leading citizens who served as worthy role models for the younger generation. Many of them also provided leadership for the organizations that nurtured social activities, promoted hobbies and special interests, and offered entertainment, especially during the long winter months. Many people looked forward to a weekly band-concert in the summer, yearly piano recitals, Christmas caroling, and a cantata presented at Easter time by a choir of about 30 or 40 singers from the town's school and its churches' choirs. A substantial brick building housing a movie theater and a four-lane bowling alley was completed on the main business street in 1940, and both enjoyed great popularity. The Rex Theater was open six nights a week plus Sunday afternoon, and it offered three different movies a week or more if counting the frequent double features. Because the school did not have an auditorium until the mid-1950s, the theater, which was large enough to seat the total school population of about 240, served that purpose and was the venue for such things as guest speakers, musical events, and the town's annual Christmas program, an offering pitched to the younger crowd. The most memorable feature of that program was receiving, upon exiting the theater, a bag full of peanuts in the shell, hard candy, and an apple from the obliging and portly gentleman-farmer, J. Roy Carter in his Santa Claus costume. In a separate and distinct event also held in the theater, the three local farm-implement dealers sponsored an "Appreciation Day" targeting farmer-clients in promoting the latest farm machinery. This gesture recognized the agricultural basis of the region's economy, and it meant an early release from school and a packed theater for the promotional films, movies, and live entertainment. During the academic year, high school sporting events drew small crowds in support of the "Ruthton Vikings," a name that reflected the town's demographic make-up and seemed not to offend the scattering of Irish, Dutch, and German residents. The town at various times also had bowling leagues, men's baseball, women's softball, ice skating, indoor roller skating, horseshoe tournaments in the park, plus fishing in the nearby lakes and streams and duck and pheasant hunting in season.

Toward the end of summer many of us looked forward to the county fairs because they offered something different and exciting: exhibits of the work products and handiworks of local folks, live entertainment, carnival-type rides, and rare culinary delights such as cotton candy. The fair we most often attended was the Pipestone County Fair. We usually drove there late in the afternoon, went through exhibits such as livestock, garden products, baking and cooking, and 4-H projects. After that Don and I would go on our favorite rides: Ferris Wheel, Tilt-a-Whirl, and Octopus. We finished the day by attending a grand production in the grandstand which featured races, clowns, music, skits, and fireworks. These varied opportunities in our town and in our corner of Minnesota for entertainment, hobbies, and social activities together with a tradition of long work hours offered little excuse for boredom.

When looking back on those "growing up" years, it seems clear that the events beyond our local, state, and national borders were quite extraordinary, and that they exerted an unusually large role in altering the course of our nation's history. Those events also shaped perceptions of ourselves and of our place within the larger context. From the late 1930s through the following two decades, those historic experiences—the Great Depression, the Second World War, the Korean War, and the Cold War—altered our lives directly and left strong imprints on our recollections of those years. The forces of depression and war inevitably impinged on our daily lives, so questions about those forces naturally arose and motivated many of us in Ruthton to become avid consumers of the news as presented through newspapers and radio broadcasts. As one of the town's three or four newspaper delivery boys for about three years in the mid to late 1940s, I know that many residents subscribed to the morning or evening daily newspapers published in Minneapolis. In our house each of us regularly read sections of the newspaper, and we listened to radio news reports while eating breakfast, as well as in the early evening, and again at bedtime. We were fascinated by the radio newscasts, especially those from Europe, presented by broadcasters we could readily identify by voice and accent: Edward R. Morrow, Eric Sevareid, Richard C. Hottelet, and Winston Burdett. This information was supplemented by RKO News films shown before each movie at the local theater and by the required reading and study of the "Weekly Reader" in school. Adult conversations often centered on the dramatic developments intrinsic to that era, and as young people hovering on the fringes of such discussions we properly kept our mouths shut, but we witnessed the passion often attached to such discourse. TV remained a novelty in most Ruthton homes until the late 1950s, so it did not become a significant source of our current-events information until the following decades.

The central value bequeathed to my generation by the Great Depression was frugality, a value that remained strong through this two-decade period. It endured partly because it simply bolstered an existing rural, small-town value. It was further strengthened by wartime shortages. One example of frugality in our home was my grandmother's practice of saving remnants of bar soap until she had collected enough to wrap and bind them in a piece of cloth so when moistened it could be used for washing hands and face for a few days. She thus saved the cost of a new bar of soap. One of the most common evening scenes in our home was my mother and grand-mother sitting in their respective living rooms for a couple of hours darning, patching, and repairing items of clothing in an effort to keep them in service for just a bit longer.

We were all fascinated by news from the theaters of war. Several young men from town and farm had been drafted or had volunteered, and their locations and status were of obvious interest. Whenever my grandparents received a letter from their youngest son, Uncle Ben, who joined the army and served in the Pacific Theater in New Guinea, our family gathered as Grandma carefully read it aloud.

One of our neighbors, Newell Lane, served as a bombardier based in England. On one of his missions over Germany his plane was shot down; he survived but was captured and served the last year or two of the war in a German prisoner-of-war camp. His fiancée, Elvina, kept the town informed of his status whenever she received a communication from him directly or from the Red Cross. At the end of the war in Europe in May, 1945 and then about three months later when victory over Japan was declared, a special day was designated to celebrate each victory; at a specified hour on those days Ruthton's three churches simultaneously rang their bells for several minutes. Don and I eagerly took our turns pulling the rope to the bell tower of the Methodist Church.

As we made the transition from the Second World War to the Cold War our interest in those external events remained high. It was impossible to ignore the many dramatic developments marking the arrival and deepening of the Cold War: the start of a series of atomic bomb tests at Bikini atoll in 1946 (some of which I heard on radio broadcasts), the blockade of land routes to Berlin by the Soviet Union in 1948, the success of the nearly year-long American airlift in breaking that blockade, the first successful atomic bomb test by the Soviets in 1949 as well as the victory of the Chinese communists in that same year, and the Soviet launch of sputnik in 1957. The fact that the military draft remained in force during those decades provided a strong incentive for our interest. I remember a conversation with "Butch" (Roger) Myers, one of my classmates, in 1952 about the Korean War (1950-1953), the draft, and what we planned to do after graduation in 1954. As it turned out, he and two friends from the class of 1953, John Nelson and Charlie Anderson, joined the Marine Corps together. For my part, I was able to defer my draft obligation until after graduation from the University of Minnesota.

Those of us who grew up in the 1940s and 1950s lived in the shadow of what Tom Brokaw has called "the greatest generation." This reference is to the men and women who struggled through the depression and who sacrificed through the war years to bring the nation to victory and to a position of world leadership. The greatest sacrifices were asked of those who served in the military, and they included our neighbors and family members. Whether they lived up to that generational label or fell short, they personified the qualities that made us feel good about ourselves and our nation—hard work, sacrifice, and humility. Their example instilled a deep sense of national pride in all of us but most certainly in my generation.

Saturday Nights

Saturday nights uptown were particularly exciting. The business section of town extended for about two blocks, and most of the stores remained open until 10 pm, while the pool hall, bowling alley, and three restaurants kept going until midnight. Saturday nights became even more lively when the graveled business street was paved after the Second World War thus permitting street dances on special occasions and the setting up of traveling carnivals such as the Jay Gould Carnival for the occasional two- or three-day period of evening and week-end fun. On most Saturday nights it seemed like the whole countryside poured into town creating a happy congestion. In reality, that was the only time during the week that some farm families came to town, and they came for shopping and socializing.

One memorable Saturday night in the late 1940s, Cedric Adams came to town. As the radio voice of Minneapolis-based WCCO, he was probably Minnesota's most widely-known personality during the 1940s and 1950s. Adams was the main attraction at a ceremony inaugurating Ruthton's just-completed ball park with its lush green outfield, freshly laid-out diamond, and large banks of elevated lights

Ruthton Business "Main Street," circa 1940

which enabled extended night play over an expansive area for the first time in the town's history. During the previous weeks some of us kids accompanied town leaders such as Ben Anderson and Jay Jackson as they drove to neighboring small towns where we handed out flyers inviting the countryside of southwestern Minnesota to join the festivities surrounding Cedric Adams's appearance and his dedication of the ball park. It was an easy sell because he originated from Magnolia, a town in our corner of the state but even smaller than Ruthton, and he had a loyal following.

This event was special for about six of us boys, aged 10 to 13, who that summer spent many nights sleeping under the trees in Robert Pike's backyard—our "campground" with pup tents positioned over sleeping bags on mattresses which rested atop wooden orange crates, all of which provided comfort and a glorious sense of freedom and independence. That freedom allowed us to walk the two blocks uptown to the bowling alley to buy a root beer float or an order of fries before turning in for the night. The evening of the dedication was different from the usual Saturday night in that the town was full of people well into the night, many of them strangers, and by 10 pm most of them were still lingering at the ball park or socializing uptown.

Directly across the alley from our "camp" was the town park with its band stand, horseshoe pit, and war memorial. About an hour before this memorable dedication day had come to an end, one of my pals came running through the park and into camp and quietly but urgently announced, "Listen, I just saw a man and woman lying on the ground near the bushes over there away from the park lights, and they're doing it!" This hurried announcement was met with the following outpouring of disbelief: "What?" "You're kidding!" "I don't believe it!" "Are you sure?" "How do you know?" After this initial shock and disbelief came the recognition of a rare learning opportunity. How could we be so lucky! Then came a plan of action. One of our proactive members quickly sized up the situation and commanded: "Okay everyone, get your flashlights. We'll crawl over there and surround them!" What a wonderful chance to get answers to some increasingly important questions as we were entering our teenage years. We're talking know-how, mechanics, the mysterious beginning of life! We quickly but quietly implemented our plan. We indeed managed to surround the entwined target, but our beating hearts and heavy breathing must have spooked the amorous pair. They calmly gathered their garments, composed themselves, embraced, ambled to their car, and drove off. From disbelief to excited anticipation to utter dismay—and, oh, so quickly! What had we missed? All those questions and still unanswered!

One factor that added to the liveliness of Saturday nights was the opening of a liquor store less than two years after the end of the war—a development not unrelated to the return of several veterans. This proved to be a controversial change that came about through a vote by the residents. This part of rural Minnesota nurtured a strong temperance sentiment that was actively promoted by some of the churches, so the vote—a close one—came as a shock to many, especially to those who had failed to vote because they had assumed an easy win for the temperance forces. The victory in favor of the liquor store came about largely because it authorized a "package" store in which alcohol was sold by the bottle as opposed to a bar where it was sold by the drink. A package store seemed more discrete. An early choice by the town council of a manager to operate the liquor store was Jens North. The selection of Jens was based on his reputation of honesty and from fear that if there developed a pattern of selling the product to minors, the town's vote could be reversed. Jens was not a young man at the time; he had had a varied career including prospecting for gold in the Yukon as a young man and more recently when he worked off and on as a carpenter. Jens appreciated this chance for steady work; he was the father of seven children including David, a friend and classmate of mine through all twelve years of school. The council's choice was a good one; he did an excellent job and remained as manager for many years.

One citizen who most certainly voted in opposition was "Little Hans" (Alvin) Hansen, and his vote was not motivated by temperance sentiments. As a young man he had been trained by his father, "Big Hans," who was the best carpenter in town—a master carpenter. He stood about 5' 7," so the names "Big" and "Little" were relative only to each other. The two worked as partners for several years with Little Hans specializing in the painting part of a project. But the partnership did not run smoothly. I witnessed the dysfunction when they did some remodeling in our house in the mid-1940s. Big Hans was modest, soft-spoken, and very skilled, whereas Little Hans was pugnacious and rather prickly. He had a habit of questioning his dad's ideas and of second-guessing him. He seemed to enjoy an argument for its own sake. For reasons probably known only to the family—but not hard to guess—the partnership ended shortly after that.

By the time Ruthton's package store opened, Little Hans had become the town's principal source for hard liquor, a reliable source but not exactly legal. However, folks generally avoided any reference to him as a "bootlegger." He was usually available and could be found most evenings in the bowling alley where he sometimes worked as a short-order cook, or where in his free time he polished his competitive bowling game. He kept his inventory neatly stored in his car trunk. During my college years in the late 1950s, some Ruthton friends and I had on one or two occasions witnessed Little Hans's practiced stealth. He would direct his customers to drive separately and meet him at some dark and secluded place at the edge of town such as the stockyard or grain elevator to transact business, probably as he imagined it was done in the Twin Cities. At the rendezvous site customers were admonished not to attract attention; for example, turn off the car headlights, talk softly, and don't slam the car doors. At that time and for at least the previous decade, Ruthton employed a part-time sheriff, a local man who worked primarily in the evenings. At least one of those sheriffs conspicuously wore a holster with a loaded six-shooter. Little Hans got the message and acted with due caution. Even after the opening of the package store, he offered his services "after hours," so to speak. No one seemed to begrudge him this sideline because he had trouble making a living as one of the town's two or three painters. He seemed accident prone, and, after a history of falling incidents, people were reluctant to hire him, so the modest income generated by his after-hours services helped meet basic needs. In reality he didn't need much income because as a bachelor he lived with his parents for decades. Little Hans thus enjoyed reliable laundry service and some home-cooked meals.

James W. Park

Seasonal Change

Growing up in rural Minnesota meant early development of a keen interest in the weather. Everyone was well informed about it, primarily through frequent broadcasts over radio stations in Minneapolis and the South Dakota cities of Sioux Falls and Yankton. In our family we always caught the forecasts at bedtime and during breakfast. The first thing we did in the morning after dressing and preparing for breakfast was to check the outside thermometer through the north window. The most useful gifts handed out to customers at Christmas time by local businesses were those ubiquitous outdoor thermometers as well as calendars which reminded us of the start and end dates of the seasons. Fall's early frost, winter's blizzards, spring's flooding, and summer's heat and humidity—all offered conversational openers, particularly in a region so dependent on agriculture. Minnesota's dynamic weather patterns and the seasonal changes could be highly dramatic—whether a bone-crushing temperature change in autumn, a severe, days-long blizzard in the dead of winter, a damaging flood in spring, or a summer marked by extreme heat.

Autumn was the most cherished season because the weather could be truly glorious, and we knew those ever-shortening days signaled an inevitable change. Another sign of that change was the southward flight of flocks of ducks and Canadian geese. Whenever we heard them honking as they passed overhead, we stopped whatever we were doing, tracked their flight, and wondered if we would be blessed with a long Indian summer. Meanwhile, the season offered the pleasantries of football and hunting. Fine dining in fall offered roasted pheasant, stuffing, squash, and a dessert of pumpkin or apple pie from the season's harvest. And then there was the first hard frost that abruptly ended the mosquito problem! The beauty of fall's colors was emphasized by the many elm and maple trees scattered throughout town and in the countryside. Kids learned to identify most of the tree varieties from science-class assignments to collect, display, and identify leaves from the local trees. We were very aware of our natural surroundings, so it was an appealing assignment. We knew there was only one catalpa tree in town—just north of the school building and next to the road—and in order to include an oak leaf in a collection you had to get out to the shoreline around Twin Lake. Directly across the street from our house were three or four mountain ash trees which were quite rare in our region and which produced beautiful clusters of reddish-orange berries every autumn. Apple trees were quite common, and we enjoyed several varieties totaling between two and three dozen trees scattered in backyards throughout town. Aside from a few plum trees that produced small but delicious fruit, apples were the only fruit tree that did well in our climate. One of the season's iconic events was raking leaves into piles along the side of the unpaved street—we had about ten trees along the front and one side of our corner property—burning them, and inviting the neighborhood kids to join us in roasting marshmallows over the dying embers. For many days in October the town was filled with the unforgettable aroma from the many piles of burning leaves.

One of winter's lasting memories was sitting in a classroom and watching the buildup of wind and snowfall that marked the approach of a blizzard and wondering if school would soon be dismissed. If we were graced with dismissal would it be soon enough for the school buses to get the country kids back home safely, and, if not, in whose homes in town would they spend the night? It was usually with the faculty members. Those unplanned overnights were not frequent— maybe once every three or four years—but the mere possibility provoked excitement. The first heavy snowfall of the season did not always come roaring in like a furious Siberian tiger. It sometimes arrived gently on cat's paws without strong wind or frigid temperatures. Regardless of its temperament upon arrival, its aftermath was transformative. How it concealed fall's brown drabness, the dead and dying vegetation, the stubbled corn fields—all hidden by a glorious, pure white, crystalline beauty that you would remember forever!

That first snowfall's beauty even transferred to the pleasurable anticipation of shoveling the extensive sidewalks around our house. The job belonged to my grandfather, Don, and me. I recall pleading with Grandpa not to start the shoveling until we boys had finished our indoor chores so we could all share the fun. He was restless to begin because he loved to get an early start on his three-block walk uptown to get the latest news from his friends, but he always waited. The snow shovels had been prepared days in advance by heating them in the basement furnace and then waxing them with paraffin to make sure the snow slid off easily.

During the winter months, Don and I kept busy at home with indoor chores, homework, reading, and playing games. If the weather was too harsh for outside play, the two of us alone or with a couple of friends played games such as Monopoly in the basement where we could also roller skate or set up our electric train. That "Marx" electric train was a fantastic Christmas gift from our parents in the mid-1940s. Dad had great fun "instructing" us in how to set it up and operate it, and we and our friends enjoyed it for many years. During weekday winter evenings we parked ourselves near the radio in our living room, our "entertainment center," and closely followed the adventures of several of our heroes through a series of 15- or 30-minute programs such as: "Terry and the Pirates," "Sergeant Preston of the Yukon," "Hop Harrigan," and the most indispensable of all, "The Lone Ranger." Even in the summer, outside playtime did not commence until the latter's 7 pm conclusion. Another fond memory from those years was our Friday night walk uptown on the crunchy snow for the usual Western double-feature movie at the Rex Theater. With any luck we could watch one of my favorites, the "Durango Kid," as he brought order to the wild West while Don and I shared a large, ten-cent bag of popcorn.

Much of our time in the winter was also taken up with music. Don and I each took piano lessons, and from dedicated practice we early on gained a level of proficiency that was satisfying. When the school formed a band in the late 1940s, I learned to play the trombone and Don the coronet; we each enjoyed our concert- and marching-band activities through high school. Starting in 1950 we took stringed instrument lessons from the Methodist minister's wife—Don on mandolin and I on guitar. I was not a very good guitarist and did not enjoy it, and after a couple of years I managed to wiggle out of that commitment. Don, however, became very good on the mandolin so that we formed a good duo with me as his piano accompanist. Our mother signed us up for about six to ten "gigs" a year—more than we wanted—for such things as PTA, Eastern Star, and wedding anniversary celebrations. Though these multiple commitments to music were pleasurable and enlightening, they left us with little free time which was, at least in part, the point of the crowded schedule.

One of the reasons we took such delight in the season's first blizzard was the possibility of the free time it offered. It normally arrived from the northwest either with a gradual but powerful buildup, or with sudden fury. You never knew the month of the season's first blizzard, its strength, or its duration. The excitement came from this uncertainty and from the rupture in routine activities—such as going to school. Notification of whether there would be school the next day was a bit tricky. In most cases we were advised to tune in to a Sioux Falls radio station for a listing of area school closings. But if the blizzard arrived during the night or if it was not a large, area-wide storm, the school-closure news was disseminated through lots of calls from the local telephone company, owned and operated by Chris and Gladys Andersen and their daughters, all of whom worked at the switchboard in their home. The news was presented as an important message from "central." Upon the arrival of the storm we measured its strength by gazing out the north-facing windows to find out how far we could see—if to the water tower, a block and a half away, not so bad; but if not even to the Methodist Church across the street, wow, a blinding blizzard!

If it was a big blizzard, Don and I ran upstairs to spend time with our grandparents, Peter and Augusta Christensen, who had lived there with their youngest daughter, Aunt Bernice, since 1939 when

Park Family Home, Built in 1938-1939 at cost of $6,000

construction of the house was completed. She was trained as a practical nurse by the town's physician, Dr. A. F. Sether, and remained in his employment until the early 1950s when she moved to Minneapolis. During the nearly two decades of growing up in Ruthton, our grandparents were intrinsic to our daily lives. An early memory at the start of World War II is of Grandpa fastening a world map to their living room wall so we could more easily track the course of the conflict. He proudly pointed to Denmark, his place of birth, and I pretended it was so tiny I couldn't see it. Grandma thought that was quite cute, but not Grandpa. Actually, they both had a lively sense of humor, and they maintained a loving relationship from the time of their marriage in 1896. He seldom mentioned his humble background or his early years growing up in Denmark prior to arriving in the U.S. at the age of 18. She, on the other hand, spoke with pride of the advantages of having grown up in a small city in Iowa, which offered a stark contrast to the rigors of life in rural Minnesota. As a proud Iowan she took offense at any negative comment about that state or its people;

in her quiet way she registered particular objection to criticism of former President Herbert Hoover, a fellow Iowan. She also spoke in glowing terms about her father and of his insistence on the highest standards of comportment and appearance. After all, he had worked for years as coachman for members of the royal family of Denmark!

I had many opportunities to observe the pleasure each of them took in their relationship. A few times when I went upstairs for a visit—note that their door was always open for unannounced visits—I found Grandpa standing on an open newspaper spread out on the living room floor while Grandma approached holding an ominous-looking sewing shears. The task at hand was to trim his long, unruly eyebrows, a service that no Ruthton barber would include in the price of a simple haircut and most Ruthton men would never ask for. "Now Mama, why not wait for a week or two? I can still see." And then came the expected retort: "We go to church tomorrow, so stop talking and stand still!" A few snips here and there concluded the performance, and we soon returned to our duties with smiles of recognition of a job well done with harm to none.

Arriving upstairs during blizzard conditions, we engaged Grandpa in a few hands of rummy—we advanced to pinochle as we got older. Part of this routine involved our periodic surveillance from the upstairs windows and analysis of the blizzard's strength over a plate of Grandma's homemade cookies. She was a good cook, especially in her baking. In honesty, however, it must be noted that there was one unappealing food item she contributed to the family feast every Thanksgiving and Christmas—at the polite invitation of Mom and Aunt Bernice: the stuffing for the bird—turkey, goose, or duck. Grandma seemed quite proud of the greyish, pasty, weakly-seasoned substance that filled the bird's inner cavity and unfortunately

Floyd Park on the Job, circa mid-1920's

overflowed it. We never complained because there was always an abundance of delicious food plus a rich gravy to cover a small helping of her stuffing. Aside from that trivial flaw, she was excellent in the kitchen, and she was a good housekeeper—she swept the stairs daily with a goose wing. Don and I also learned in our younger days that she was a proficient reader; she would gladly read to us before bedtime from our book of Grimm's fairy tales. So, those strong blizzards strengthened family ties, and they brought tangible benefits such as school vacations and mountains of fresh snow for making igloos and digging tunnels.

Another reason for the central importance of the weather to my family was that for more than forty years my father was Ruthton's rural mail carrier with a route of about 100 miles at the time of his retirement in 1963. In winter it was a tough job—especially in December with all of its Christmas cards and packages. The work day began by 7 am and sometimes continued until after our 6 pm supper time. I witnessed the work first-hand a few times when he let me ride with him on days when school was closed because of the snowfall—the very thing that made his job a challenge. For me, sitting in the back seat as he was driving the rural route was a great delight as he tried to blast through the snowdrifts blocking the country roads, getting stuck, backing out, shoveling, and giving it another go at high speed! I vividly recall one of those moments when the two of us were alone together in the car and I decided "innocently" to try out a new word I had learned from one of my older friends, Jack Christensen. Sitting in the back seat ready to hand Dad the correct package from among those piled beside me, I reached for a large one and said, "Here's a really big bastard!" "What? What did you say?" I softly repeated it, and he asked, "Where did you learn that word?" I explained that I had picked it up from Jack and that I did not know what it meant. He calmly declared it a bad word, explained its general meaning, and admonished me not to use it again. "Oh, okay."

Mail delivery had been much more challenging in earlier decades because of the poorer roads and equipment. For a few weeks early in 1927, heavy snowfall kept the roads blocked, so Dad had to use a team of horses and a sled to negotiate his route. A decade later for two consecutive winters he confronted the same problem, but in this instance he "modernized" by buying a specially designed "snowflier"—a model A Ford body mounted on two rear axles with lugs like a caterpillar and a pair of heavy-duty skis replacing the front wheels. With the snowmobile, no need for roads to get around, but you did need snow! The following few winters brought normal snowfall, so the snowflier was never again used. I remember playing in it when it was parked in our garage where it remained until Dad sold it for scrap iron during the first year of the Second World War.

Both Mom and Dad were mindful of the importance of always having a reliable car. The family's livelihood depended on it, and both were cautious drivers. But the rugged conditions of many of the country roads delivered a terrific beating to the car, so Dad had to trade for a new car every year or two. It was always a Ford or Chevrolet. Because he did not enjoy the process of negotiating—haggling was not part of his nature—he would first go to the Chevy dealer in Tyler and then to the Ford dealer in Pipestone and then buy from the one offering the best deal. That was the sum total of his negotiation. He felt comfortable with the process because, as he once explained, he trusted the dealers. A couple of my friends expressed amazement at such an uncommon level of trust—actually, they expressed their surprise a bit more crudely! Their disbelief led me to raise the question with Dad, but his refusal to haggle accurately reflected his marked belief in the integrity of others.

Dad serviced the car regularly—at Al and Ed's Standard Oil Service Station in Ruthton for routine maintenance or for more serious work at the dealerships in Pipestone or Tyler. A couple of times when Don and I were very young Dad took us with him to Tyler for a two- to four-hour servicing job. Our reward upon completion of the job for not overly complaining about the long, boring wait was to go directly from the dealership to a Tyler restaurant where we each ordered a chocolate malted milk served in a tall, silvery canister overflowing with goodness. What a treat! We usually got home just before dinner time, and Mom was more than a little annoyed that we had no appetites for the meal she had prepared. Dad knew better than to make a habit of such indulgence.

After getting my driver's license at age sixteen Dad and Mom sometimes gave permission to use the car for an evening event. On one such occasion I drove, with Don as my passenger, to a musical program in Pipestone. In the twilight on the way there, a pheasant suddenly flew up from the side of the road, slammed into the windshield on the driver's side, and cracked it without breaking it. My immediate thought was, "Wow! What will Dad say?" When we returned home after the program, which I can hardly recall, I apprehensively described what happened. Dad went outside, looked at the damage, and said: "When something like that happens it's easy to lose control of the car and have an accident or end up in the ditch. It could've been worse. Good for you!" I slept soundly that night.

Preparing the house for winter involved, for some families, little more than replacing the window screens with storm windows and making sure the coal bin was full. I recall in the early 1940s when Perry Scroggie, the town drayman, delivered coal with a wagon pulled by a team of horses. The coal was loaded manually at the lumber yard's railroad siding, delivered by wagon to the target house, and shoveled into a metal coal chute that passed through the basement window and into the coal bin, creating a terrific racket and a cloud of coal dust. But many houses were not insulated and they lacked storm windows and central heating. In such cases a common practice was to stack bales of hay against the foundation all around the house and, in lieu of storm windows, use wooden lathing to attach a special type of heavy waxed paper over the windows to keep out the wind. Some homes, even in town, lacked toilets and indoor plumbing thus requiring use of a bucket or a frigid trip to the outhouse, several of which remained in active use in the 1940s. The family of one of my best friends in the pre-school and first-grade years, David Svenning, had an outhouse that he and I and his family used whenever it was more convenient than making the trip into the house. I considered it a deluxe outhouse, that is, a two-seater, because we could sit side by side, chat, and kill spiders while doing our business. After cleaning up with whatever kind of paper happened to be available we were ready for action.

By late February we were all so tired of winter that we were eager for the first real thaw of the season even knowing that the sloppy, slushy conditions were certain to last several days—but, oh, the relief! Whether February was a month of 28 or 29 days, it couldn't possibly be the year's shortest! An early sign that winter could not last forever was Anna Mae Jackson's offer of a nickel to the first child in town to spot a returning robin. Another indication that spring was coming was the arrival in town of Whistling John. As I remember him he was a hermit, some 60-plus years of age, who lived on a small farm near the railroad tracks about three or four miles south of town. He spoke little in his Swedish accent; he wore heavy boots, bib overalls, a sheepskin overcoat, and a cap with earflaps, and he was missing several teeth. Whistling John kept a few goats—he had trained goats for a vaudeville act in his younger days—and he reportedly lived off the land by hunting and trapping. He somehow survived the winter relying for warmth on a pot-bellied stove in his small shack. It was thus a special event when he sensed we were far enough into spring to chance the long trek into town. He was always friendly to us kids, and every spring during those rare and brief visits he took the time to show us how to make whistles out of willow branches at that special time in spring when the sap was beginning to flow. So the arrival of the first robin and of Whistling John were welcome signs that we were into another seasonal change—the most warmly embraced of all.

Looking back at our winter-time experiences in Minnesota, it seems that we took much pride in enduring, year after year, the rigors of that challenging season. It was as though the mere act of living through those winter months had somehow strengthened our character. Very simply, we felt good about ourselves when, with the arrival of spring, we would hear someone exclaim, "By golly, we made it through another winter!"

Though welcomed with relief and joy, spring's true character was one of turbulence and indecision. The year's heaviest snowfall often came in the last half of March which created a high probability of rapid thawing followed by major flooding. The threat of tornados was an occasional feature of late spring. I recall a few times when I stood with adults on the western edge of town and looked anxiously to the southwest at the approach of threatening tornado clouds. Though the threat was large, Ruthton was always spared major damage. Late spring also brought excellent fishing in the region. Many families in town and on the farm were avid gardeners, and this was their season. Before its end we could take pleasure in freshly baked rhubarb pie with ice cream as well as shortcake just out of the oven loaded with strawberries or raspberries from the garden.

A degree of seasonal tranquility often seemed to accompany the arrival of summer, but this is not to deny the occasional thunderstorm, hailstorm, or tornado threat. The joy of outdoor work and recreation seemed somehow to trivialize such significant weather events as mere interruptions to the dominant theme of the delight bestowed by decent weather. We also welcomed summer because it brought a sense of freedom from the constrictions of boots, hats, overcoats, and gloves, and it freed us from indoor confinement whether in school or in the house. In most years by July we were embracing the restorative powers of summer's sun. But there were exceptions. I remember more than one summer that never seemed to warm up. When you had to wear a sweater at high noon on the Fourth of July —that was no summer! In such years we were thus-denied the customary pleasure of complaining about the excessive heat and humidity. It is difficult to overstate the comfort and pleasure delivered by the normal Minnesota summer. It was during the early years of elementary school when we learned about the seasons and their starting and ending dates; I will forever recall the dismay I felt when that lesson about the seasons made me realize that the start of summer, June 21, was also the longest day of the year and that for the next six months the days grew relentlessly shorter. It seemed so unfair.

Fishing and Hunting

The standard for successful fishing was set by those anglers who knew how to land walleyes and northern pike. Fishing for bullheads in the local waters was common sport for folks from Iowa who drove up for two or three days of camping and fishing at our two local lakes and for beginners such as Don and me. Bullheads were relatively abundant, easy to catch, and very tasty early in the season when the water was still cold. Another delicious fish available in the larger, local lakes was the crappie, closely related to the sunfish but larger. It was easy to catch near shore, and it had white, flaky meat. Dad introduced us to fishing in nearby lakes and streams when we were in our pre-school and early elementary school years. We became eager fishermen after mastering the fine arts of baiting the fishhooks with fat earthworms from our garden, casting, patiently waiting for a strong nibble, and reeling in the catch or in some cases a tree branch! On many occasions Don and I would dig for the worms before Dad got home from work in the hope that he would be free to drive us to a lake for a bit of late afternoon fishing. More often than not, when we demonstrated our seriousness by showing him a coffee can full of worms, he was agreeable.

The closest local lake, about four miles north of town, was Twin Lake, also known as West Twin or Big Twin. Its "sibling" was too small for good fishing most years. Within about an hour's drive we had at least three other lakes that were usually good for fishing—Lake Benton, close but rather shallow; Lake Sarah, distant but with good fishing; Lake Shetek, about an hour's drive to the southeast. Lake Shetek's size and depth offered the best fishing in the area for varieties of game fish. It was also a recreational lake with provisions for boating and camping, and it was used for extended stays by groups such as the Boy Scouts. High school classes sometimes celebrated the last day of school with a chaperoned trip to Lake Shetek by school bus.

Twin Lake was large enough for bullheads and perch but not deep enough to sustain walleyes and northern pike. A road followed the shoreline around about a quarter of the lake and provided easy access, and there were trees of many varieties along nearly all of the shore. Most fishermen fished from the shore rather than from a boat. But the many trees created problems for casting, and tree limbs that had fallen into the lake often snagged the fishing lines. The local Sportsmen's Club periodically addressed these problems by tree trimming and by clearing fallen limbs from the water near shore. I fished there along the east shore many times as a young boy with Dad and Don, and in my high school years the lake's north shore was a favorite swimming spot after work and on week-ends. It is also where I learned the rudiments of water-skiing along with a lot of other guys. This came about when Ed Krall, John Deere Implement dealer, bought his sons—Gary, Ron, and Cork—a beautiful Chris Craft wooden power boat. The Krall boys were one, two, and three years younger than I, and we were all good friends. They were generous in letting me and many of their other friends learn, through trial and error, to water-ski with their Chris Craft. All in all, Twin Lake was a great site for specific recreational activities or for just fooling around.

To have a good chance to catch the prized fish you had to travel to the larger lakes of northern Minnesota or Canada. But such dedication was for the real enthusiasts. And Ruthton had several. Usually in the fall after the first hard frost—hard enough to kill the mosquitos—a group of six or so men would assemble for a week-long fishing expedition to the North, often into Canada. Members of the group varied but involved a core group of townsmen—John Huhnstock, Ben Gaudian, and Mel Johnson—and farmers—Walt Ausen and Adolph Lofthus—and it always included one man who knew how to cook hardy meals. In some years Little Hans was the cook of choice. One of those years when he had been a member of the fishing party, he happened to come over to our house to talk to Dad about a painting project. This was shortly after the fishermen had returned from Canada, so the conversation immediately turned to his account of it. "Did you catch many fish, Hans?" queried Dad. "Did we catch many fish? Why, Floyd Park, you wouldn't believe how many fish we caught!" came the gleeful response. "Was the weather very good, Hans?" "Was the weather very good? Why, Floyd Park, you wouldn't believe how great the weather was!" he answered with animation. And so went the conversation before our attentive family seated in the living room. That fishing expedition was probably one of the year's highlights for Little Hans.

This annual fishing trip was much talked about both before and after the fact, sometimes with envy because most people were unable to take a whole week off "just for fishing." When the fishing party returned with their filleted fish on ice they were met by family and friends in the parking lot behind both Johnson's Fairway Grocery

Store and the next-door pool hall and between the rear of those buildings and the alley. This open area was large enough for many people to gather, welcome the returning fishermen, examine the catch, and comment. It was apparent that this unkempt and unshaven group of campers had had a relaxing time of serious fishing and probably nights of poker accompanied by the appropriate beverages. Ice chests empty of booze but packed with their catch offered testimony of a "spirited" week.

Hunting was also an important part of our culture, and we were introduced to it at a very young age. A few folks enjoyed it into old age. Though a good fisherman, Dad was an indifferent hunter, but he taught Don and me the basic skills of both. During pheasant-hunting season in the fall, Dad would drive us when we were young boys along the country roads in search of those elusive birds. We seldom spotted them close enough for a decent shot, but late one afternoon we saw a large rooster a short distance ahead in the ditch beside the road. I spotted him first, and Dad slowly drove up next to the target. As he stopped and prepared the gun, the bird slowly strutted, then crowed, and then. . .wow, a perfect shot! Our first pheasant! That early experience with Dad left a lasting, positive feeling about hunting in general, even though our success rate was quite low. In fact, when we three hunters returned home with our trophy bird, Mom was more than a little shocked. By about the age of ten many of us boys made sport of shooting rats, gophers, or rabbits with .22 rifles. But the greatest hunting experience for us as teenagers, by which time we had graduated to shotguns, remained pheasant hunting. Whether sweeping through a cornfield as part of a large group or joining with two or three friends stalking the birds, it was exciting and often rewarding, for, after all, Ruthton lies in the zone of pheasant-hunting paradise.

On the far upper end of a hunting experience that touched Ruthton was moose hunting. To my knowledge the one and only successful moose hunter was the town's noted blacksmith, John Huhnstock. In 1939 he had taken over the shop from his father, Henry, who then moved on to start a successful plumbing business. Henry was widely respected for having served as mayor for several years and as town sheriff for a time, for taking charge of paving the business street, and for accepting responsibility for maintaining the town's infrastructure including roads and water system. In addition, it was his hand that pulled the lever at noon six days a week that set off the loud siren signaling dinner-time, thus helping the town maintain regular order. Huhnstock's Blacksmith Shop was located on the corner of one of the two intersections of our business street, a prime location. Its large open doors and noisy activity summoned visitors to gather around the forge and banter with John whose standing in the community was burnished by his father's reputation. In his own right he acquired quite a following. This was partly because he was an active sportsman and one of the regulars of the fall fishing expedition to the North and because of his leadership in the volunteer fire department. John was about 5' 10" tall, muscular and solidly built, and he earned a certain notoriety because he differed markedly from most men in Ruthton in that he was ruggedly individualistic, outspoken, and shamelessly profane. He was respected as a skilled blacksmith, did quality work as a welder, and in those jobs he faced little competition—hence the rough treatment he meted out to some of his customers. Everyone knew you could not push him around or rush him. If you needed your lawn mower sharpened in preparation for the coming summer, you had to get it to him by mid-winter, look for someone else to do it, or sharpen it yourself. Despite his noted gruffness, he was also capable of unpublicized good deeds. John Huhnstock was a large presence in the community, and it was difficult to ignore him.

One autumn in the late 1940s, instead of going north with the usual fishing group John went moose hunting, and after a few days he returned with his trophy in the back of his truck. To everyone's surprise he managed to suspend the poor beast from a sturdy limb of the large maple tree just outside his shop. This busy intersection offered the perfect location for careful study by all interested parties. Our path to school took most of us kids directly past the moose, and we often saluted it, gave it a sympathetic pat, and offered comments about its heavy coat and big ears and questions about its gender. This was in late fall when temperatures were below freezing, so no problem with a rotting carcass. Days, and weeks, and months went by, and everyone in the county had a chance to admire John's prize and to attend "the viewing." When friends or relatives from out of town came for a visit, a drive around town usually ended with an examination of the moose suspended from the maple tree and a chance to take a few photos with family members next to John's prize. As the spring thaw approached, inevitable questions about a proper burial arose, as well as the larger question of the point of it all. The longer that symbolic trophy—symbolic, perhaps, of John's manhood—remained hanging from the tree, the more questions it generated. After a few weeks folks such as my grandfather began making comments such as, "I think John forgot about his moose," and "At this point it probably doesn't taste so good." Finally, before the spring thaw, John ordered a truck from the rendering works and had his trophy lowered and hauled away for disposal. To the best of my knowledge that marked the end of John's moose hunting, and it marred his heretofore unsullied reputation as a sportsman.

Religion

One of the shaping influences while growing up in a small farm community was its religious profile. In a population of about 500 souls the overwhelming number were Lutherans followed by Methodists, Dutch Reformers, and about five or six Catholic families. The Lutherans were further divided along ethnic lines, primarily Norwegian and Danish, both of whom had separate churches in town. The lesser-numbered Swedish Lutherans faced difficult choices: find a distant Swedish Lutheran Church, mingle with the Danes or Norwegians, or go for neutrality and join the Methodists. The largest country church whose members shopped and attended school in Ruthton was Ellsborough Lutheran Church located about eight miles east of town. It was Norwegian, and the most prominent families in its membership were the Ericksons and Larsons. Methodists supported the town's third church, while Catholics, Dutch Reformers, and German Lutherans traveled to nearby towns for services. Jews were nonexistent in Ruthton in my time, but my grandparents spoke with warm affection about their family physician from an earlier era, Dr. Golden. Religious activities represented an important share of the town's social and cultural life. In addition to Sunday services and

Sunday school, the churches also sponsored youth organizations, week-long summer Bible school and/or camp, frequent church suppers, special programs for the public at Christmas and Easter times, and guest speakers.

Methodist Church and Parsonage

The pastors of the town's three churches were well educated and highly esteemed men. They were much endeared partly because they had bonded with their parishioners through the hard times of the Great Depression and the early years of the Second World War. Thereafter they were reassigned more frequently, particularly in the case of the Methodists. This was of importance to me because my family was Methodist following my father's faith. In fact, his father was a founding member of our church, and Dad honored that tradition by his strong faith and his conduct. He served as church treasurer for several decades, and during much of that time my mother was superintendent of an active Sunday school program. When they married she left the Danish Lutheran Church and became a Methodist, later declaring that the Methodists were in greater need of help. Dad also performed a unique function in that he presided over the first portion of the Sunday morning church services until the minister arrived from two charges earlier that morning, one a country church west of town and the other in the small town of Verdi. So, as the minister's "stand-in" over the decades, his presence in the pulpit offered a sense of continuity for a congregation subject to a frequent change of ministers.

Sundays in Ruthton were special for nearly everyone. For many it was a day of worship, but because nearly everyone put in long days, six days a week, it was a much-needed day of rest. For our family, Sunday morning began when we all sat together at the breakfast table and Dad led us in a few minutes of devotions. We were then free to enjoy a delicious breakfast including fresh baked goods. On Easter Sunday morning we indulged in a tradition which was part of the Pennsylvania Dutch heritage of Dad's mother. We had a breakfast centering on eggs slowly poached in a rich cream sauce in a heavy iron skillet and served on top of bacon or ham over toast. It was remarkably satisfying and savory! Following breakfast, Don and I sprawled out on the living room floor and read the several pages of the Sunday comics. Reading the funnies became a life-long ritual for Don—I have been less faithful to it—and it began when Dad passed the reading task over to us kids shortly after we learned to read. The importance of the comics was evidenced by a moment around 1947 when the Mayor of Minneapolis took to the radio to read the Sunday comics to children in Minnesota hospitals suffering from that much-dreaded disease, polio. That mayor was Hubert H. Humphrey. After chuckling over the comics we were in a good mood for attending Sunday school and church services. An unusual "ritual" of Sunday school was for the superintendent to ask if any of the children had gotten new shoes during the preceding week. If so, the obligation was for that child to deposit two cents in a special collection box. When enough money was collected it was used to buy a new pair of shoes for a child living on a Minnesota Indian reservation. The purchase of new shoes was a noteworthy occurrence in those days, and this Sunday school practice probably began during the depression years.

Our reward following church was a large, delicious Sunday dinner typically featuring a pot roast, mashed potatoes with gravy, vegetables, and the total menu highlighted with homemade dinner rolls and pie. Following Sunday's dinner, Mom's edict was that Don and I were responsible for doing the large stack of dishes and cooking utensils. There was no escaping this chore.

Those baked goods were but a part of the plethora of tasty items that poured forth from our kitchen every Saturday morning, often the output of an approximate four-hour joint effort of both my mother and grandmother. It was for this that Mom always bought flour in fifty-pound bags and stored it in the kitchen's large flour bin. Some of the baked treats to emerge from the kitchen were seasonal such as a much-anticipated pie made in May and early June from the abundant rhubarb in our garden. By noon on a typical Saturday a warm, inviting aroma infused the house with the soft, spicy sweetness of fresh baking, and our family was set for the week with supplies of cookies, pie, nut bread, dinner rolls, and sweet rolls.

Dad wore a mantle of unquestioned faith in his Christian beliefs. He read the Bible regularly and prayed daily. His sincerity, integrity, and warmth of character were respected by all in the community. An example of his good will came in his treatment of our nearest neighbor, Jens Nelsen, whose property abutted ours, but it lacked a garage for his car. In Minnesota's winters a garage is as important as snow tires. We had a two-car garage but generally used only half of it. Jens, a good neighbor but not a close friend, approached Dad about renting the unused half and offered to pay a generous amount. Dad felt embarrassed to accept the proffered amount but finally agreed to accept $5 a month! And so it remained for many years. An incident relevant to Dad's character, but unknown outside the family, began one afternoon in the late 1940s with a discrete knock on our front door by a stranger. After a brief conversation with Dad, the stranger indicated that he and Dad needed to have a private conversation, so they drove off together. About an hour or so later Dad returned alone and explained that he had just met with an IRS agent who questioned him about his recent tax returns. The issue concerned the amount claimed for charitable contributions on his returns which he always filled out himself. The proof offered was the many canceled checks he had saved and which he subsequently showed to the agent, checks written to various charities but primarily to the Methodist Church— case resolved!

I did not share Dad's strong religious convictions, and in my last two years of high school I tentatively began to express my doubts in a way that did not directly confront his beliefs. Sometimes after the Sunday church service I would challenge an element of the sermon, hoping for an argument about the illogic of such things as talking serpents. He remained calm, showed great patience, and offered a reply such as: "It's a matter of faith not logic." What a deflating response when I was hoping for a debate. I found it quite maddening that he could be so certain of himself while I was consumed by doubt. Despite my questions over matters of faith—an issue central to Dad's life—his love and support never faltered.

During the 1940s the Methodists adapted to five different ministers. The most noteworthy and impactful was Reverend William J. Davidson who served during much of the depression period and into the early 1940s. He left a noteworthy legacy because he arrived at a time when the church was faced with the prospect of closure because of declining membership and the approach of bankruptcy. By force of character and a personal charisma he revived membership and restored the church to solvency. He, his wife, and their three children blended well into the community and endeared themselves even to non-members. In fact, he held office as an elected member of the Ruthton Public School Board for a few years in the late 1930s. He had a common touch to the extent of helping with the physical labor involved in refurbishing the parsonage, and his family shared in the general poverty of the period. One afternoon while playing outside near the parsonage when I was about five years old, Mrs. Davidson invited me in for a glass of milk and a cookie. As she opened the kitchen cupboards to fetch a cookie I was shocked to notice utterly barren cupboards except for a lonely bag of store-bought cookies. The contrast with the abundance of food in our kitchen was unsettling, and I recall reporting this discovery to my parents whose general response was that there were lots of people in Ruthton who were "struggling." This was also one of the many times I heard them say in an appreciative way, "We have it good." After Reverend Davidson was reassigned to a church in Le Center, Minnesota, church members from Ruthton kept in contact with him and on occasion drove to Le Center for a one- or two-day visit. He and his wife, in turn, sometimes returned to Ruthton for brief visits.

On one of those visits around 1945, Anna Mae Jackson took advantage of his presence by having him officiate at a small service for the purpose of having David, her grandson and one of my best friends, baptized. She and her husband Jay were raising him, and the three of them lived in an older house near ours and near the Methodist Church. They were an interesting and intelligent couple with firmly-held opinions, and they were non-church-goers by conviction—at least no one in Ruthton ever witnessed either of them enter a church. But Anna Mae had been sending David to the Methodist Sunday School for a few years, and she felt that for David's sake he should be baptized. Because of her warm regard for Reverend Davidson, she felt confident that he would perform the service in a meaningful but simple and discrete manner. So the baptism was held in our living room where friends gathered as witnesses to the brief ceremony presided over by Reverend Davidson. A final recollection of him is of his final visit to the Ruthton church several years later following his retirement. He spoke at a Sunday evening service to a large crowd gathered in the church sanctuary. Everyone sensed this would be a final get-together, and the closing hymn was "Blessed Be the Tie that Binds." It was a memorable and deeply moving experience filled with abiding affection, one for another.

Another minister of the 1940s, Reverend G. W. Powell, was a short, elderly Englishman with a pronounced accent and a powerful voice. As he worked his way toward the climax of his Sunday sermons he could be quite thunderous. In fact Aunt Bernice commented a few times that she didn't need to attend church because she could hear him from her upstairs bedroom across the street with her windows closed. Reverend Powell was unfamiliar with the use of a saw, hammer, crowbar, or snow shovel and could not drive a car, but he had a young, attractive wife who was comfortable in the driver's seat. Within a month or so of their arrival Dad and Mom invited them to our house for dinner where the fancy table cloth and quality setting on the dining room table suggested a higher than normal degree of formality. Early in the dinner as the platter of homemade dinner rolls was being passed, the minister took one, passed them on, and suddenly dropped his roll on the table. Because it had such a perfectly rounded form, it went rolling down the table, miraculously avoiding all obstacles until it finally lost momentum and came to a rest where all saw it and stared at it. I am not certain what happened next because we were all distracted, bemused, and struggling to maintain a degree of decorum and sobriety. Mom may have grabbed it and brought it to the kitchen where she probably admonished it, sterilized it, and saved it for later use! In truth, this minister was not one of her favorites. This perhaps freed her to gleefully retell that story in future years whenever Reverend Powell's name came up. But it's worth noting that she seemed never to repeat it in Dad's presence. This early introduction to the minister suggested that he was going to be an odd fit in a community of laboring folks, and he was not to be trusted with sharp tools beyond a knife and fork. But any negative comments about him usually ended with a remark such as, "But he sure can deliver a powerful sermon!"

Another incident related to Reverend Powell happened one afternoon when I was running across the street between our house and the parsonage. His playful cocker spaniel, a recent gift from a parishioner, chased after me, bit my finger, and, as I jerked my hand away, I ended up with a bloody gash in my finger. A few minutes after learning of the incident, the minister came out on his open porch carrying a croquet mallet, grabbed the dog, and proceeded to beat the poor animal as I stood in guilty silence across the street with my bandaged finger afraid to say a word in the dog's defense. The strong, repeated poundings and the helpless dog's yelping made it an unforgettable scene and led me to wonder, "Did that poor dog get the point of such a beating?"

A few years later the Methodists hosted their fifth minister of the decade, Reverend T. Benton Clark, and he remained for four years. He was a man with a level of humility appropriate for a small farm community, a quality not shared by his wife who seemed aloof and rigid and who presented herself as an accomplished violinist. As it turned out, she was a fairly good violinist and was able to offer music lessons on violin, guitar, and mandolin. Within two years she was able to bring a few young people in the church—including Don and me—to the point where we could play in a five or six piece stringed-instrument ensemble. On occasion the Reverend and his wife would spend an evening at our home, so we became well acquainted. They were enthusiastic and accomplished Chinese checkers players and were often able to cajole two or three of us into playing a few games with them. They played like tigers, usually won, engaged in no chit-chat during play, and showed no Christian charity in their competitive spirit. But otherwise the Reverend was a man of joy and good humor. His Sunday morning duties required him to conduct services at two other Methodist churches before arriving at our Ruthton church. His very first sermon in Ruthton was based on the Old Testament story of Jehu, the Israeli king who was noted for slaying his heathen adversaries and for racing around the countryside at undue speed in his chariot. Our minister made this story relevant by admitting that he felt like Jehu in his drive to get to each of his charges in time to fulfill his duties. He chuckled warmly at his own story, and his levity was not considered amiss.

In the early 1950s three or four families in Ruthton showed us the future by early purchases of TVs even though such devices were useless most evenings because transmission sites in Sioux Falls and Minneapolis were so far over the horizon that the images were mostly obscured by heavy, wavy, electronic snowfall. Nevertheless the local Red Owl Grocery Store sponsored a contest offering a free TV set to the person submitting the best, most appropriate poem. Reverend Clark won with the following lines:

I'm a preacher man of little means.

I don't raise oats, I can't raise beans.

I don't play cards, I never bet.

That's why I need a TV set.

If only this happy story ended here. Unfortunately, TV reception in Ruthton of barely adequate quality required an antenna at least 30 feet tall that could be rotated manually or electrically. Such an addition was more costly than a TV set itself, and most Methodist ministers lacked such funds. So, what was the poor poet to do? He requested that the Church Board purchase the antenna and make it a permanent installation on the parsonage. The request was turned down, but into the breach stepped a church member who had had a good year on his farm, enjoyed the parson's rhyming talents, and who thus made the purchase. That generous member was Morris Minett, a gregarious, popular farmer who was well known throughout the region for his specialty in drilling wells as a sideline to farming. Morris was also generous in sharing the musical talent of his four children who, as a quartet, sang popular and folk music to guitar accompaniment at various church programs. A year or so after Reverend Clark was reassigned to a larger parish, I heard a prominent member of the community make the observation that the minister's most enduring legacy was that very tall TV antenna, the Morris Minett antenna, attached to the Methodist parsonage. That was an unfair comment because he was best remembered for his robust sense of humor and for his grace in presiding over weddings, funerals, wedding anniversary celebrations, and the baccalaureate service for my high school class upon our graduation.

Beginning in the 1930s and continuing at least to the mid-1950s the Methodist Church was noted for hosting a group of visitors from the Deep South every two or three years. The group consisted of five or six singers, faculty and students, from Rust College, a Historical Black College founded in 1866 by the Freedman's Aid Society of the Methodist Episcopal Church. It is located in Holly Springs, a small city in northern Mississippi. They traveled by car or station wagon and presented an evening program in the church to which the public at large was invited. The church sanctuary was always full, and the crowd seemed generous judging by the look of the collection plate which was passed for the benefit of the singers and the college. The program consisted primarily of Negro spirituals and traditional hymns, and their rendition was unique and impressive. What a contrast their lively and heartfelt presentation made to the restraint of our customary Methodist renderings. Of the spirituals offered, the crowd's favorite at every program began with the line, "Dem bones, dem bones, dem dry bones." Following the formal program we all adjourned to the basement for a variety of delicious "eats." I have a vivid memory of at least three of those programs beginning with that of 1945 or 1946. That one was especially memorable because at the outset I was intrigued to see a black person up close for the first time in my life. I think my reaction was guided by that of the congregation in the sense that we saw ourselves as gracious hosts, co-religionists, and Northerners welcoming them to this respite from the severe restrictions of the segregated South. The last of those three visits that I can recall was in the 1950s during the ministry of Reverend Clark. As the singers were preparing to walk down the aisle at the end of the program, Reverend Clark approached them, gave each a warm hug, and to the women a kiss on the cheek. There was no mistaking his message of respect and deep affection. I was moved by the beauty of the entire event, and others in the audience also seemed to recognize that it was a very special occasion.

From the late 1940s through at least the mid-1950s, a group of about fifteen to twenty teenagers participated in a church-sponsored organization, the Methodist Youth Fellowship—the MYF—which met weekly in the church basement during the school year. It maintained a loyal following because of the skills and personalities of the leadership team, Edna Olson and Dorothy Nirk. They shared a good mix of contrasting personalities and an understanding of teen-agers; in fact their own children were members of the MYF. This was a supportive organization for teens because it offered an opportunity for forming close friendships outside of the larger school context and for developing social skills. The regular meetings had a religious patina—the minister seldom attended—and the time was spent on discussions, games, songs, and snacks. Now and then we enjoyed a special event such as Christmas caroling in the neighborhood or going on hayrides in the autumn. The hayrides involved climbing aboard a hayrack provided by a farmer-parishioner and getting comfortable in the thick layer of sweet-smelling hay. A tractor then slowly pulled us along a few miles of quiet country roads for a couple of hours. On one of those hayrides our guest was the high school science teacher who taught us about the constellations and planets as we lay on our backs gazing upwards while enveloped in the deep darkness of the countryside away from the town's lights. The number of shooting stars we were able to count in that short time amazed us. We sometimes talked about scheduling a hayride to coincide with that autumn spectacle, the northern lights, but its appearance was too uncertain.

I was able to gain some insight into the town's differing religious sentiments from living closely with my maternal grandparents. My grandfather, Peter Christensen, was born in Denmark, arrived in New York as a teenager, was naturalized in Iowa in 1896 when he swore "to renounce forever all allegiance . . . to the King of Denmark of whom he was heretofore a subject." My grandparents faithfully attended Ruthton's Danish Lutheran Church. The four-block walk to church was a bit too far for my grandmother, so Dad would give them a ride whenever possible. When he couldn't drive them, our close neighbors, Jess and Emma Larsen—fellow Danish Lutherans— were helpful and happy to give them a lift. There was never a doubt about the strength of my grandparents' faith, and it was confirmed in my mind one day when I was about 6 years old. I was quietly walking upstairs for a visit when I saw my grandmother on her knees beside the bed praying. I quietly retreated so she never knew she had been seen. It reminded me of a Norman Rockwell painting of a Thanksgiving scene. Our family often attended events at their church—suppers, anniversary celebrations, and Christmas activities. I was always impressed by how warmly the minister greeted us on those visits. At their Christmas service I vividly recall the minister following what seemed to be a long-standing tradition of reading parts of the famous Hans Christian Andersen story, "The Little Match Girl." It always struck me as a terribly sad story to inflict on the congregation at such a joyful time. But at my young age I no doubt took it all too literally.

We Methodists also noted what we considered the more casual attitude of the Danish Lutherans on religious matters. For example, they occasionally took much of the summer off from Sunday school. Such seeming laxity was anathema for the Methodists. The contrast was even more striking with the ardent Norwegian Lutherans who at times hosted a guest speaker who had previously been a Catholic priest and who enlightened his audience on the issues that had led him "to see the light" and to abandon his Catholic faith. Note that several Catholic families—mainly of Irish and German backgrounds—lived in Ruthton.

Theological doctrines and religious practices normally offer distinctions among churches, but in Ruthton those differences were also delineated by the cuisine offered at the frequent church suppers and holiday celebrations. The Danish Lutherans proudly offered varieties of delicious baked goods. Among the most prized was Danish kringle. One food that distinguished Danish cuisine was aebleskiver, available only on certain occasions in special locations such as the Fourth of July in nearby Tyler, a largely Danish community. This delicacy resembled a waffle in texture and ingredients, was the size of a small tennis ball, often contained apples or other fruit, and was topped with syrup, jam, or powdered sugar. The Swedish Lutherans throughout Minnesota had an enviable reputation for their smorgasbords. This all offered a contrast with the Norwegians and their lutefisk suppers! I must take the liberty to note, however, that the church suppers also featured some items typical of the Midwest which I found rather unappetizing: creamed, canned corn; scalloped corn, pickled beets, and jello which often lacked even a hint of added fruit to give taste and substance to the quivering mass!

My experience with Ruthton's three churches suggested that all were in the mainstream of Protestant theology and practice, that is, they were conventional and somewhat lacking in the evangelical fervor found in parts of the rural Midwest. Our Methodist Church underwent a partial deviation from that conventional profile when a newly-assigned young minister arrived for a short stint in the mid-1950s. After a few weeks of settling in, one Sunday morning following his sermon he urged those in the congregation who were "saved" to come forward, kneel, and accept his blessing. During the ensuing two or three minutes of stunned silence in the auditorium, I scanned the assemblage, held my breath, and firmly gripped the pew! No one moved. Finally, a lady who was faithful in her attendance got up, strode forward, and kneeled. She was considered a hard worker in the church, but her gruffness and lack of tact were distinguishing qualities. Two or three other members followed her forward. I was fairly sure Dad would not move, but I waited and waited. . .and I was right. He didn't budge. Oh, what a relief! I believe he felt it was inappropriate to convert an inherently private matter into such an ostentatious gesture. In subsequent weeks the minister issued this invitation one or two more times, and then gave up on us. In my recollection the only other hint of an evangelical bent in our church was in the mid-1940s when I went with our minister, my parents and brother, and several other church members to Marshall, about a one-hour drive north of Ruthton. It was at the urging of our minister that we attended what was called a "Singspiration" held in Marshall's large school auditorium and featuring a choir and preaching by Billy

Graham at a time when he was just starting to make his mark. It was our one and only Singspiration.

Although the religiously-affiliated residents represented the town's large majority and shaped the moral tone of its culture, they shared the terrain with many who were without such affiliation. This latter group contained several people who were respected, including the editor of the weekly newspaper, at least five business owners, and Otto Erlandson, manager of the town's locker plant. The Erlandsons lived a block from our house and had four sons. The youngest, Chuck, was five years older than I, preceded me as a stock clerk in Johnson's Fairway Grocery Store where he was much admired by his boss and all of his coworkers. After I started working there I learned how difficult it would be to live up to his work ethic. As a student in his last year of dental school at the University of Minnesota he provided great advice and encouragement when I was preparing to enter the University. The Erlandson family, as well as many others without church ties, were well regarded and integrated into the town's social life. I never heard a negative comment about any of them based on their lack of formal religious attachment. This observation invites the question of whether there was criticism of those with specific religious ties. The answer is that it was uncommon, but it existed and it was directed toward Catholics, sometimes with humor and on occasion with an unkind bite.

Ruthton's moral order was upheld by nearly all members of the community, and it was grounded in the religious precepts taught by the churches in town and in the surrounding area. One memorable event of the early 1950s offered an interesting challenge to that moral order. It began at a Christmas holiday party for school faculty held at a teacher's house in town. The basic elements of the unfolding scandal were: the flow of holiday "spirits," the early, quiet departure of two of the teachers, both married but not to each other—"Mr. Coach," high school teacher, and "Mrs. Teach," elementary school teacher—a quick stop uptown for a six-pack of beer, and a final stop at Mr. Coach's empty house. Meanwhile, the two abandoned spouses remained at the party, but when it ended Mrs. Coach returned home and came upon what must have been a traumatizing scene which led to words and actions that invited attention from neighbors. Detailed news of the scandal spread and led to speculation about the School Board's likely action. The Board met shortly thereafter and decided to allow the two teachers to continue their assignments until the end of the school year so there would be continuity for their students. In June their contracts were terminated; both quickly left town, and they never returned. This scandal inevitably brought shame to the two families directly involved—Mrs. Teach's family was broken by divorce—and shame to the school and the community. But after the initial shock, the predominant sentiment expressed by most residents was sorrow, and they seemed to accept the Board's action as appropriate. There was certainly moral outrage at the egregious conduct by supposed role models, but the community's reaction was calm and pragmatic. About two years later I had a chance encounter with each of them separately in Minneapolis. Mrs. Teach and I suddenly came face to face and exchanged awkward words one day while walking on the University of Minnesota campus—I was a freshman and she had returned to school for graduate work. I ran into Mr. Coach in Bridgeman's Ice Cream Parlor in downtown Minneapolis where I was taking a break from an afternoon job search, and he was chaperoning a group of high school seniors. We both managed to behave as though we were old friends.

School Days

It was an odd elementary school custom, and it no doubt lasted well beyond those years in the mid-1940s when my classmates and I joyfully participated. It usually took place late in the school year when spring's pleasantness was imparting a more relaxed outlook than we had felt during the long slog through winter. Also, by April or May we had adjusted to the rules and oddities of another new teacher, had learned the extent of her flexibility, and had grown to respect and like her. I say "her" because in each of those six years all were women, and all were good teachers. Just how widespread a custom it was I have no idea, nor do I know when or why it began. But there it was, the ritualistic "peanut shower."

In secret preparation, students would agree on a date, time, and start signal, usually a book dropped by a designated student for initiating the "surprise" peanut assault on the teacher. When arriving at school that morning, students secretly brought and hid in their desks, lunch bags full of peanuts in the shell, an inexpensive snack sold in bulk at most grocery stores. The unwritten rule was to throw a few or a handful of peanuts at a time at

Ruthton Public School

the besieged teacher who was scripted to act surprised, defense-less, and good humored during the oncoming cascade. And why not, for the day's work was essentially concluded except for the janitor, Alfred Petersen, whose workload had just been doubled.

One might wonder about the attitude of the school principal concerning such a seemingly disruptive event. I recall on at least one occasion when he quietly entered the back of the classroom, seemed bemused by the chaotic scene and soon left without comment. In his eyes, our teacher probably appeared to have established solid rapport with her students. Indeed, she had, for when ammo was exhausted the teacher emerged from behind or in some cases from under her desk and invited us to spend the day's final hour enjoying the bountiful snacks scattered all about us.

The twelve-year journey from the start of first grade and on to graduation in 1954 was a joy. Of the twenty-four graduates in the class of 1954, eight of us made the entire trip together. Five of the eight were from town, and the other three lived on close-in farms. We townies learned more from the farm kids than vice versa, and the things we learned were important for anyone living in a small farm community—for example, the differences in the looks of a field of oats, barley, or wheat. Despite the ongoing learning, it was not until my high school years that I came to understand the difference between straw and hay. There were basic values that we also learned from each other. Our first-grade teacher encouraged and supervised outdoor activities including nature walks, sports competitions, and races such as "pump, pump, pull-away." One such random event in the spring of that first-grade year was a competitive race among all interested classmates. I was fast, and I knew it, and

James Park and David Svenning -
First Day of School , 1942

I was confident. We lined up, the teacher blew the whistle, and about eight of us took off on about a 30-yard sprint. And the winner was— Norma Mattson! How could it be? Beaten by this short, slender girl, and in front of the entire class. I had run as fast as I could, and yet I lost to a girl. It was a violation of the natural order in my mind, and I never quite forgot it. For Norma, the ever-friendly, popular girl from town, there was no gesture of triumph, merely a broad smile as though her win was a routine matter.

My first three years of elementary school were the war years, 1942-1945. The shortages and hardships brought on by the wartime economy were not so different from what people had experienced during depression years. The difference was that they were formalized by government and made official through rationing and use of tokens and coupons for basics such as food and gas. An example of shortages in school was paper towels. Each class had an appointed student monitor to make sure that when our teacher escorted us for our restroom break down the hallways in two separate files, one for boys and one for girls, no one used more than one paper towel in the restroom. Other items unavailable or in short supply were rubber products such as boots, overshoes, and inner tubes—all of which had to be repeatedly patched to remain useable. To replace a car tire you had to convince a rationing board at the county seat of a compelling need. Unavailable products included Christmas tree tinsel and lights. By Christmas 1944 we had only one working bulb for our tree, and it was white. Dad attempted to color it blue by dunking it in a bottle of ink, but we ended up with a white bulb with blue blotching. We also participated in "paper drives"—collection by the Boy Scouts of newspapers and magazines—and we made sure to save things such as tinfoil and flattened tin cans. Meat products were severely rationed, and turkeys were unavailable, even for Thanksgiving or Christmas. The common understanding was that they were all being reserved for the troops. Sugar was sharply rationed, and it became a particular problem in our family because we possessed a large, collective sweet tooth. We were not making it through the month with our official allocation. So, Mom cleverly announced a policy whereby we would each start out with a pint jar, labeled with our names, full of sugar. All four jars were conspicuously lined up on the kitchen counter. Within a few days it became apparent that Dad was the family's "sugar monster" because of the generous portions he used on his cereal and in his coffee. Don and I offered to "subsidize" his sugar habit, but Mom declared such sharing to be a violation of the rule of equal portions. Mom got the result she was looking for: Dad stopped using sugar in his coffee, and the problem largely disappeared. Fortunately, Ruthton had a commercial beekeeper who provided a partial solution to the sugar shortage. Many residents made regular trips to the "bee barn" and altered baking recipes to make the switch from sugar to honey.

Many families responded to encouragement from federal officials to help the nation avoid a serious food shortage by expanding their vegetable gardens thus creating what became known as "victory gardens." We had always had a garden in our backyard, but during the war and for a few years thereafter Dad got the okay from the Methodist Church to convert its unused grassland and weed patch on the north end of the church into our family's victory garden. This was a substantial piece of land for a family garden—at least 1,000 square feet—and it supplemented our existing backyard garden. And it was close to our house—across the street and behind the church. Its size allowed us to plant several rows of sweet corn, string beans, and potatoes as well as smaller amounts of a few other vegetables such as cabbage and tomatoes. All of us, including Grandma, spent time working in this garden—planting, cultivating, pulling weeds, and harvesting. Don and I had it easy; we mainly pulled a few weeds and picked the potato bugs off the growing plants. The biggest chore at harvest time was digging up the potatoes and carrying them home by the bucket. We then brought them downstairs to the basement where they were stored in a large pile in a corner for the winter. Mom also put in many hours canning the abundance of corn and beans. By the end of summer the basement shelves were full of canned food, though the great bulk of it was fruit rather than these homegrown vegetables. The canned fruit, primarily peaches, apricots, pears, and plums, was purchased by the crate in Johnson's Store as it came into season. Mom referred to these canned fruits as "sauce" and when combined with homemade cookies this became a frequent supper-time dessert.

One war-related practice that became part of school life was the drive to raise money to buy U. S. Government War Bonds. Students in each classroom were encouraged to bring dimes and quarters to class on specified Fridays as a contribution toward the class's purchase of a war bond. Posted at the front of the classroom was a chart depicting a Japanese warship at sea, and on those special days the money collected was totaled and equated on the chart to the incremental sinking of the warship deeper and deeper into the ocean depths—a vivid lesson in the need for collective action in the war effort. Don had a similar experience in his class on Wednesdays. When collections were completed, the class sang the following ditty:

> We buy our stamps on Wednesday
>
> To win the war, to win the war.
>
> We buy our stamps on Wednesday
>
> To work and win the war.

A school-days recollection would be remiss without a comment about an ever-present parental concern over childhood illnesses. It is easily forgotten, but during our elementary school years most of us suffered from measles, mumps, and/or chicken pox—I had all of them—and we were often bedridden for many days at a time and missed a lot of school. Houses were posted with quarantine signs for diseases such as diphtheria and scarlet fever which occurred but not as commonly as those three mentioned above. Health issues seemed a special concern during the war years. Apples, oranges, or tangerines were occasionally handed out by the classroom teacher for purposes of improving nutrition. At times the teacher would require us to display our hands, front and back, atop our desks, while she made the rounds and checked for cleanliness; those failing the test were sent to the restroom with orders to scrub hands, fingers, and nails. Vaccinations and booster shots were given for some childhood illnesses, and I remember entire classes walking the two blocks to Dr. Sether's office to get the required shots. Following the inoculations, at least in some years, we returned to the waiting room and then marched into Dr. White's dental office, housed in the same building, for a quick check-up.

These winter-time illnesses explain our mothers' obsession with dressing for the weather—coats, caps, scarfs, gloves, and overshoes— and for taking our dreaded daily dose of cod-liver oil during those cold months. What really got the moms upset was when we arrived home for supper with wet shoes and socks. This often happened in winter because we loved to play on the ice covering small ponds, especially on a type of rubbery ice that we sometimes got in springtime or during a mid-winter thaw. The challenge was to bounce gently on it without cracking it and falling through. And we sometimes failed!

If we complained too much about such precautions as the cod -liver oil dosage, Dad would sometimes tell us how illness, especially influenza, was warded off in his family when he was a boy. His mother required the children in the family to wear an "acifidity bag" containing a foul, fetid-smelling herbal potion, an asafetida, around the neck as a disease preventative when going to school or into town. When probed for more details about this family practice, Dad seemed rather guarded, but he implied that when forced to wear such a bag he and his siblings were the objects of ridicule from friends and classmates. It seems that the Park family was noted for this practice before it became more widespread as a result of the 1918 influenza epidemic and its high death toll. At that point the odiferous bags became available for purchase in some pharmacies.

Oddly enough, it was polio, "a summertime disease," that was for us in the 1940s and 1950s the most dreaded of all contagious diseases. One reason for our fear was the mystery of how it was contracted. It seemed to be contagious primarily among young people and to occur most frequently in summer. As a preventative measure the Pipestone public swimming pool was sometimes closed during extended hot spells in July and August. Aside from the mystery of contraction, polio was dreaded because it often led to severe paralysis, in some cases to the extent of virtual imprisonment inside an iron lung because of a paralyzed diaphragm. Full recovery seemed rare, but efforts toward improved treatment were well publicized in school, movies, and news outlets. The March of Dimes was founded in the late 1930s and was actively promoted by President Franklin D. Roosevelt who was a victim of polio; this fact was not generally known to the public nor were we aware of the extent of his paralysis. The March of Dimes became a vehicle for spreading information about polio and for funding the battle against it, and in Minnesota the opening of the Sister Kenny Institute in Minneapolis in 1942 for treatment and rehabilitation for its victims further elevated our awareness. In elementary school I recall at least two occasions when classes walked to the theater to watch a film about the work of the Kenny Institute. In addition, in Ruthton we all knew someone who was a polio victim— Clarence Jensen in my parents' generation and June Peters in mine. June was in my brother's class and lived a block from our house. She contracted polio in the late 1940s and received extended treatment in Minneapolis, but the polio left her substantially paralyzed in both legs. Clarence and June were everyday reminders of polio's toll.

By the time of our high school graduation the twenty-four of us in the class of 1954 had formed close bonds. One event that helped keep us together was the annual celebration during our high school years of the combined birthday party for two of our most popular classmates, Carmen Pilegaard and Robert Udstuen. Both had been members of our class since entering first grade in 1942. Carmen had everything going for her—looks, intelligence, and personality. She was active in many of the school's extra-curricular activities, most prominently as cheerleader for several years. She, more than anyone in our class, worked to make sure that all of our classmates were encouraged to participate in class events and were warmly welcomed to them. Robert was the most popular guy in the class because of his sense of humor and his joy in life. No party involving our class was complete absent Robert. He possessed a quality musical voice, was a fine dancer, and because of his strength and girth he handled the very cumbersome tuba in the marching band with ease. Though he may have been unaware of it, he provided some of us in the class with a metric for measuring the caliber of teachers new to Ruthton at the start of each school year. Our simple, informal test noted the number of days it took a new teacher to pronounce correctly Robert's last name, Udstuen (ood stewn). Some required many days to master it, but one teacher ranked above all others. That was our seventh- and eighth-grade math teacher, Mr. Krzisnic. For obvious reasons he was sensitive to the spelling and pronunciation of last names. That simple test proved to have good predictive value. Mr. Krzisnic turned out to be an excellent teacher. On the other hand, there was our government teacher, Mr. Pfeifle, who required repeated times to get it right. A generous judge would rate him below mediocre as a teacher, starting with the tone he set in the classroom. For example, he showed no embarrassment in announcing at the start of class on a few occasions that the class on that day would be very relaxed because he was suffering from a hangover.

The Carmen and Robert birthdays were close together in mid-winter, so if there was enough snow on the ground we would begin by gathering at the "Holland Hills" located about five miles south of town. These prominent but gently sloping hills, an unusual feature in our prairie landscape, offered the chance for skiing, sledding, or inner tubing down the slopes. After a couple of hours on the slopes we reassembled at the Pilegaard Farm Implement Dealership in town where Carmen's parents, Carl and Nancy, had cleared the shop floor for lessons and practice in dancing to old-time music. Some of my classmates were good dancers, but Carl and Nancy taught me and other beginners the basic steps of the circle two-step, the schottische, the old-time waltz, and the polka. We concluded the celebration with supper centered on chili or sloppy joes, salad, and birthday cake with ice cream.

One of the consequences of those parties during the last two years of high school was the beginning of Thursday night trips undertaken by a group of four to six classmates, guys and gals, to a popular dance hall in the small town of Hatfield, about twenty miles south of Ruthton. This had been a popular dance location for decades; in fact my Uncle Howard and Aunt Bess had danced there to the music of Lawrence Welk in the 1930s. Thursday nights were especially popular in our area because old-time dance bands were featured, and they brought in some of the best: Whoopee John Wilfahrt's Polka Band, the Jolly Lumberjacks, and the Six Fat Dutchmen. Some in our group attended regularly, but I joined them only about once a month. On one of those early adventures my date was Joyce Peterson, a cute girl with a bubbly personality, who was a cheerleader and a good dancer. By the time our group arrived in Hatfield I was stricken with the flu and spent the evening out of action and prone in the back seat of the car. After that misfortune I felt too embarrassed to ask Joyce for another date, but we remained good friends through high school.

By my senior year in high school and during the summers of my college years I also became acquainted with two other large and popular dance halls close to Ruthton. One was the Playmor Ballroom in Pipestone, and the other was the Showboat Ballroom in a beautiful location near the water's edge in the town of Lake Benton. All three regularly hosted the above mentioned old-time dance bands, and all advertised throughout the area and seemed to draw good crowds. I never got over my surprise at the many times I ran into Ruthton couples, young and old, at those venues and at how good they were on the dance floor. A favorite dance that drew everyone onto the floor was the circle two-step which required you to partner up randomly with the person next to you when the music stopped. Thus I learned that Myrtle Olson, a somewhat overweight, single woman of Aunt Bernice's generation was very light on her feet and a terrific dancer. Folks were attracted to those ballrooms because everyone seemed to have fun, the music was great, and it was not expensive for a full evening, at least if you did not overdo the beer consumption.

The final opportunity for an all-class get together prior to graduation was the traditional "skip trip" to Minneapolis by school bus in May, 1954. We spent one night in a downtown hotel—we boys had two large suites. Most of us guys refused to waste our precious, limited time sleeping so we spent it exploring the downtown area, enjoying restaurant dining, and visiting Bridgeman's Ice Cream Parlor a few times. The following afternoon we attended our first 3-D movie before returning home. I have only a dim recollection of the movie because we were too exhausted from the lack of sleep to stay awake in the theater. The skip trip was a great experience, especially for classmates who had never before been to the Twin Cities.

I would give a mixed rating to the quality of the education I received in the Ruthton High School. It was above average in English and the sciences but below average in history and government. An exception to that generalization regarding history was our World History teacher, Mr. Bill Potts. He maintained classroom control with ease, knew and loved the material, and taught it with joy. In addition I learned firsthand as a member of the school octet that he was a talented vocal-music teacher. In the community he was considered rather unconventional for his bold decision to drive a convertible Studebaker—summer and winter! All four years of English were taught by Mrs. Helene Ekse who was outstanding, and the best in science was the chemistry class taught by Mr. Tom Andrews. Whether teaching grammar or Shakespeare Mrs. Ekse was enthusiastic, quite dramatic, and mindful of including everyone in the task at hand. One reason the chemistry class stood out was that Mr. Andrews set high standards, and the class combined some of my junior-year classmates with a sprinkling of the best students from the senior class, students such as Merlin Hansen, Beulah Nelson, and Lois De Grote. My only regret about my secondary education, both at the time and thereafter, was the lack of any foreign language classes, although I remember a discussion among the faculty during the year prior to either my ninth- or tenth-grade class of the possibility of starting a German or French class. But the interest was insufficient to launch such an offering.

The general attitude in Ruthton toward using a foreign language in public was quite negative, and all of the social pressure was in the direction of suppression. For example, my grandparents were fluent English speakers, and they could speak Danish, but they refused to use it in front of my brother and me. Once in a while when my arrival upstairs surprised them, I heard them speaking Danish, but they quickly switched when they saw me. The town had very few residents who did not speak English, but one was my Aunt Clara's Danish-born mother, Mrs. Jorgensen. She and her family were active in the Danish Lutheran Church which was incorporated in English in 1936. Within a few years its designation was changed to Hope Evangelical Lutheran Church, and the option of attending a Danish-language service was dropped. Although English was the commonly spoken language in Ruthton, many residents spoke it with heavy accents. Such accents came primarily from one of the Scandinavian languages. A small number of older residents had a German accent, but even during World War II there was little or no animus directed toward them, a positive contrast with attitudes during World War I. Dad told me of an incident from the era of that earlier war when a carload of men from Pipestone arrived in town one evening and gave the front of the small house next to the Methodist parsonage a quick coat of yellow paint. Its occupants were German born.

Standards of conduct in the community and in the school were well defined and generally observed with notable exceptions such as the incident described at the end of the previous section. This is one reason why student discipline seldom became a major issue. In addition, fear of being sent to the principal's office struck terror into all of us, and then there was always the even greater danger of a notification to our parents of misconduct. Though some teachers allowed a degree of laxity, the majority firmly controlled their classrooms. The teacher's occasional outburst of genuine anger facilitated that control by creating a pall of sullen obedience. One example was in my seventh-grade social studies class taught by Howard Olson, a stern, unsmiling teacher new to Ruthton. The class met in the library, a small, narrow room in which the students were seated on both sides of a long table. Next to me sat Gordon Pedersen, and directly across the table from us stood Mr. Olson. Gordon was a friendly guy from an extended family of farmers living a few miles north of town, and his main interest in life seemed to be to continue in the family tradition of farming. The class met during the first period, and one memorable day as the teacher droned on about the day's lesson I sensed that Gordon was starting to nod off. Suddenly, Mr. Olson stopped droning, leaned forward with clenched fist, reached across the table, and whacked Gordon on the top of his head with his knuckles scaring the daylights out of everyone while declaring, "Don't you ever dare fall asleep in my class again!" We were all rendered numb while Gordon attempted to gather himself in his painful embarrassment. Rare though it was, this kind of incident gave further assurance that student misconduct would not be an issue in Ruthton. Incidentally, when Gordon reached the age allowing him to drop out of school, he did so.

Looking back at the makeup of the school's classes during the 1950s in the wake of consolidation with the rural districts, one feature of that profile was the stability in class membership over the years. About eight of us made the voyage together as classmates from first grade through high school graduation, thus the high attendance at our class reunions. Upwards of 60 percent of the students came from the surrounding farms, and most attended year after year until graduation. That stability existed partly because the great majority came from farm-owning families, but even in the case of tenant farmers, many were able to rent the same land for extended periods, thus allowing those students to graduate from Ruthton.

When my cousins—Ethel, Clara, and Charles Park—enrolled in Ruthton's secondary grades in the early 1950s, their parents, Uncle Ray and Aunt Lydia, were tenant farmers. When the family leased a farm south of town our cousins gained access to the Ruthton Public School and looked forward to the prospect of some consistency in their education. They had moved frequently within Pipestone County and neighboring counties and always with the hope of finding a more productive farm. We visited them periodically at their varied rental locations, some of which were remote and beyond the electrical grid. At those farms lacking electricity we gained some understanding of the imperative of working from dawn to dusk, the precautions necessary in using kerosene lanterns, and the importance of relying on wind power for pumping water and charging batteries. Another thing we learned was the character of that family of six—the oldest of the four children, Donna, chose not to join her siblings in attending school in Ruthton. As tenant farmers they shared the difficult lot of many of those unanchored rural laborers of that era: low income and an uncertain future. And yet they always seemed hopeful of a better future.

The lives and backgrounds of my cousins' family provide a perspective on their character and on life in rural Minnesota during the depression years and the following two decades. Aunt Lydia grew up on a farm, and she and her siblings walked a considerable distance to and from their country school. They often returned home for lunch at noon, but on cold, winter days their neighbor, George Hansen, whose farm was midway between their home and the school, invited them to stop at his place for lunch. Over the years George and Aunt Lydia's family developed a trusting relationship. Many years later after Ray and Lydia married, were raising their family, and were tenant farming in the area, George became a victim of the depression and lost everything. My aunt and uncle invited George to move in with them and help them through hard times in exchange for food and shelter. He remained with them for the rest of his life, and my cousins came to regard him as their uncle. In addition to helping with the farm labor, especially at planting and harvest times, he helped the kids with their chores and took them to ball games and movies. George hired out to neighboring farmers and shared his earnings, whether cash or goods such as a baby calf, baby pigs, or meat from a recent butchering. Over time he became a critical member of the household, particularly after Uncle Ray lost two fingers from an accident in the husking bed of the corn picker. That farm accident made certain chores very difficult, such as milking cows, and George was there to provide the needed help. When Ray and Lydia retired and moved into a small house in Pipestone, George remained with them and stayed until near the end of his life when stricken with cancer. Lydia took care of him at home as long as she could, but because he was a World War I veteran he was able to move to the Sioux Falls Veterans' Hospital for his final days in the late 1960s.

Following the end of war in 1945, interesting changes in school and in town, some big and some small, began to enter our settled way of life. I remember the day Alfred Petersen, our elderly, arthritic school janitor, came into our classroom carrying a long step ladder and some fluorescent lights. He struggled up the ladder, struggled to switch the new for the old tubes, and when that failed he struggled to install a new starter switch, all of this while we were mesmerized by the physical effort as well as by the challenge of the new lighting technology that had been installed throughout the school. Also in this immediate postwar period, one of my classmates, Gordon Pedersen, came to school showing off his new writing pen which he called a "ballpoint" and claimed it would eventually replace the fountain pen and make it, ink, ink wells, and ink blotters obsolete. I was unimpressed, having recently been given a beautiful Esterbrook fountain pen for Christmas. But within two or three years, the convenience, growing availability, and low price of ballpoints won the day among students and a bit later in the general population.

An important change in school personnel also took place in this postwar period when Newell Lane was hired as head janitor to replace the retiring Alfred Petersen. Newell was well suited for the position and remained in it for several decades. As mentioned earlier, Newell was a returning war vet who had spent the last part of the war in a German prisoner-of-war camp. He was well respected in the community not only because of his service but also because he was a very sober, vigorous, no-nonsense kind of guy. He was up every morning by 5 am so he could get to school early to make sure the boilers that provided the steam heat for the school were working properly. He lived near us, and I saw him nearly every day either in school or when he walked by our house at his usual fast clip on his way uptown. One hot evening in the summer when I was about twelve or thirteen, I was sitting on the back steps enjoying a slice of watermelon and watching Grandpa mow the lawn—note that we had a sizeable lawn and no power mower. Suddenly I noticed that Newell was walking by in his usual hard-charging way. Without stopping or slowing down, he looked at me and said, rather loudly, "What a shame! That poor old man—working and sweating in this heat while you just sit there!" And then he was gone. Stunned by the sudden rebuke, I got up, walked over to Grandpa, and insisted that I finish the job. He offered no resistance. I felt the stigma, long-remembered the embarrassment, and hoped there were no witnesses.

Another change, little noticed by town folks, was the gradual disappearance of Alfred Andersen's harness and leather-goods repair business, though he still kept busy with shoe repairs and the sale of ammunition and hardware items. At the same time the local grocery stores were making the transition in their customers' methods of payment and shopping. Payment for purchases changed from a monthly charge account option to "cash and carry," meaning that you paid by cash or check at the time of purchase. This change also came with a more general system of self-service shopping whereby customers passed through the aisles filling their own shopping carts. Before that change the shopper would go to Madsen's or Johnson's store, hand a list of items to a clerk and then proceed to the meat department or the bakery section, or browse in the dry goods section looking at boots, overalls, work shirts, or sewing material. In the meantime a clerk would gather the items on your list: a can of Butternut drip grind coffee, a box of Kellogg's Krumbles, a large can of Crisco, four boxes of raspberry-flavored Jello, two cans of Spam, a small tin of sardines from Norway, and a tube of Ipana toothpaste. The clerks worked behind a long counter and gathered these items from a bank of shelves containing the most-commonly sold products. The shelves extended nearly to the ceiling, and the clerks accessed the uppermost shelves using a long ladder that moved easily on a metal railing or by using a long pole with a grasping device on the upper end. This change in grocery store shopping was considered quite dramatic at the time but was not resisted.

When Andrew Beck tore down his ice house in the mid-1940s, he did it without fanfare, but the changes signaled by that action were also significant. Elimination of the ice house came at a time when most folks in town had already switched from "ice boxes" to refrigerators. Following that change, grocery stores started making room for frozen food cabinets, and more and more families began adding home freezers to their list of essential home appliances. Prior to those changes the ice house was the sole reliable source of ice in Ruthton during the months when Twin Lake was ice-free. On those special "homemade ice cream days," such as birthdays, Dad with Don and me would drive uptown to the ice house and buy a block from Andrew, put it in a gunny sack in our basement, and crush it using the flat side of an ax. After packing the crushed ice around the metal canister filled with the creamy mixture, we three took turns for about an hour cranking the ice cream maker until the contents stiffened to a thick, rich texture. Mom's recipe for vanilla ice cream was terrific. The flavor was superior to the "store bought" with the possible exception of cherry-nut ice cream containing maraschino cherries and pecans—a product of Nelson's Ice Cream Company of Pipestone.

Freedom

Looking back on my late pre-school and elementary school years in Ruthton, the amount of freedom we kids had to just fool around in town and in its environs is surprising. That sense of freedom and the quest for it began early. I have only a few memories from when I was about two years old and living on my grandparents' farm about two miles south of town. Most of those recollections were pleasant such as walking hand-in-hand with Grandpa down the lane to check the mailbox and watching gophers dig in the pasture, but there was a bad one from that day when I fell into the cow gutter. All in all, I felt good about those two years when my parents and I lived on the farm. In 1938 we moved to town into a rented house across the street from the lot where our new home was being built—it became "the corner house where Floyd and Eva Park and the boys live." We moved into it a year later along with Aunt Bernice and my grandparents, who had lost the farm. One summer morning when I was about four years old, I felt the urge to visit the farm, and I got the opportunity when my mother and grandmother were busy in the basement doing the weekly laundry. I walked the short distance to the highway which passed through town, headed south on the shoulder out of town on my way to my first home. In my mind I knew that I had to go to the first country intersection, turn right and continue to the railroad tracks from where I could see the farm. It was a simple route and easy to remember. I got maybe a half mile out of town when a black car pulled over just ahead of me, and the lady driver got out. She seemed to know me and asked where I was headed. I told her my destination, she offered to give me a lift and then proceeded to drive me back home where she spoke to my mother. Next week on laundry day Mom put me in a harness attached in the back to a cord which ran to a moveable metal ring on the clothes line. After a couple of weeks of the harness trick, Mom found an alternative to that dastardly harness—she asked Grandpa to spend time at home with me on laundry days in case I got that wandering urge. I don't recall ever again attempting that trek, at least not at such a young age.

Late in the afternoon on one of those seemingly endless summer days when David Svenning and I were about 6 or 7 years old, we planned to walk through the alley behind Uly Spangler's house and quietly pick a couple of apples from one of his trees. Uly was somewhat of a curiosity—in the first instance because of that rare first name, rare, at least for Ruthton. He was a man with few friends, a bachelor, and a retired painter who lived alone in a large two-story house on an expansive lot which allowed for a substantial garden and a few apple trees. To protect his abundance of apples from the always-hungry kids in town he fastened a box to one of the trees and on the box was a hand-painted sign, "Poison." It may have scared off the less sophisticated, but not David and me! As we approached his property, an unusual commotion from the front yard caught our attention. Uly had some tall American elm trees on his property, and a few weeks earlier a storm had taken one down. He had spent many days cutting it up and saving the larger limbs for winter's fuel. On this particular afternoon an elderly farmer acquaintance had joined him in an effort to load several of the trimmed logs onto the running boards of an old Model T Ford so they could be hauled out to the farm for cutting with a circular power saw. It was a big job dragging the logs to the car, stacking them horizontally three or four high on the running board, and securing them with ropes. The men exchanged few words, and David and I watched, partially concealed and in silence. In what seemed like a revelation hitting all four of us nearly simultaneously, it became apparent that, as the men were tying the final ropes to secure the logs, they had left no access to the car's interior. Crawling through the windows was impossible, particularly for two weary old men! David and I sensed their anger and frustration, felt genuinely sorry for them, said nothing, and quietly stole away. It's worth noting that about fifty years later while walking through the Ruthton cemetery I came across Uly's headstone and made a mortifying discovery—he was born in 1871 when Ulysses S. Grant was President, hence that rare first name.

David Svenning and I were best friends at the time we were watching those stymied loggers. We were the same age and close neighbors. He lived across the street from me in a large two-story house with attic and full basement. Access to the basement was down the stairs from the kitchen or directly from the outside through a large, storm-cellar door which made it easy at the end of summer to bring in such vegetables as potatoes, beets, or onions for winter storage. It also offered quick access to the safety of the basement in the case of tornados and secret entry for David and me when we wanted to enter the house undetected. The house was situated on a lot a half-block in size and with a barn and that previously mentioned "deluxe" outhouse. David lived with his parents, grandmother, an older brother and sister, and he enjoyed the company of a cat and a dog, "Fletcher." David's father was a veteran of World War I, and he kept a collection of war souvenirs upstairs in the barn. Despite his repeated warnings, we boys could not resist secretly playing with some of those items including gas masks, knives, bayonets, and ammunition. We repeatedly got in trouble defying his orders on this matter and also for playing with and teasing the one or two goats the family kept tied up in their apple orchard at the far end of the lot. They periodically led the nanny goat into the barn for milking, so David and I naturally tried to milk her and ride her when no one was about, but she had a bad temper. This too got us into trouble with David's dad who was a very patient man. Our worst offense was to wander over to the nearby dairy one afternoon when the owners were absent and proceed to throw rocks at the windows of the chicken coop, breaking most of them. We were identified as the culprits within twenty-four hours, and our parents jointly decreed that we would not be allowed to play together for one month. That was a friendship that got me into more trouble than any other. David and I were a toxic combination. Perhaps our problem had been too much unsupervised time in those pre-school years. Fortunately for both of us, we were not able to move toward adulthood together. Shortly after those interesting but troubled times, David and his family moved to southern California for work in the aircraft factories, and following the war they returned to Ruthton. Within a short time, David's mother died of cancer, and David and his dad moved to a city near Minneapolis.

A year or so after watching those old Ruthton loggers, I experienced what I thought was the happiest day of my life. My dad agreed to buy me a bike—a used one because new ones were unavailable during the war. He bought it with a check for $24—a whole lot of money—from our neighbor who was moving out of town. It was a "Sunracer"—the best bike ever built, or so I imagined. I was already a proficient rider, and over the next several years my friend David Jackson taught me how to take care of it: take it apart, reassemble it, lubricate it, adjust the chain, seat and handlebars; and install lights and reflectors. We even relocated the bike's basket from the handlebars to behind the seat for greater stability, and for winter biking we experimented with a type of chain for the tires fashioned from wire. With that bike came a wonderful sense of freedom and a growing camaraderie with about five or six guys, each with his own bike, but none with a Sunracer.

On our bikes we could easily ride to the gravel pit south of town where we dug caves—totally oblivious to the hazard of being buried alive—carved out bike trails, and trapped birds in their sand-cliff nests. We could ride to the prairie north of town and shoot gophers or to the town dump and shoot rats. We could ride to the stockyard, quickly lift up the scattered, wooden grain doors, and chase the rats as they fled. We could go to Jensen's barn and play in the haymow or ride to Twin Lake to skip stones over the water and fool around along the shore. Any of these things could easily take the whole afternoon, a time of splendid independence from adult supervision. That spirit of freedom, however, didn't mean that we felt no restraints. Often, over supper Dad would say something like: "Bertha Thompson mentioned that she saw you and three other guys riding past her place this afternoon. Where were you headed?" Though we lacked direct supervision, we were being observed.

My second great desire of that time, one endorsed by Don, was for a dog. A much-cherished vision was to explore the countryside on my bike with friends accompanied by my dog. A few of my friends such as David Svenning had dogs, and our neighbor, Jens Nelsen, had "Dexter," a friendly Boston terrier. But Dexter was usually kept on a short leash so he could get only as far as our common property line. One late afternoon as I was playing in our garage, I noticed through the garage window that Grandpa had just arrived home. He climbed the back steps to the house, noticed Dexter watching him, looked around to see if anyone was observing, and then stomped his feet. Dexter responded with indignation—loud, prolonged barking and howling! A short time later when I entered the house, Mom said, "Grandpa just complained again about the loud racket the neighbor's dog makes. Poor dog, tied up for hours. Town is sure no place for a dog." That was the oft-repeated argument against my pleas for a family dog. Parents and grandparents were united in their joint position: "Dogs belong out on the farm where they can be helpful and can roam around freely." That argument was bolstered by an incident involving a week-end visit by my Uncle Howard, Aunt Bess, and Cousin Myrna who lived in St. Paul. All in our Ruthton family were downstairs to greet them when they drove up. We held the front door open, and as they began entering the house, this smallish, short-haired brown dog launched herself from the back seat of their car, dashed up the sidewalk, shot up the steps, through the living room, the dining room, and into the kitchen where she skidded on the linoleum floor, regained her bearings, circled back into the dining and living rooms where scatter rugs scattered, suddenly came to a halt under the beautifully-set dining room table, and emptied her bladder on the carpet. This was our introduction to "Christina" who provided the definitive answer to my campaign for a family dog.

The Rez

An unusual feature of Ruthton was the existence of a reservoir, the "rez," created by the railroad through excavating land and building a low rock and dirt dam across a creek along the north edge of town. It was built within a few years of completion of the railroad in 1888 to provide a reliable source of water for the several steam locomotives that daily passed through town. The rez was about a mile out of town, accessible by foot but not by car. Its semi-privacy was secured by the surrounding farmland and the heavily wooded acres abutting the rez itself. All of its qualities—the deep, cool, slowly running water, the seclusion, and the proximity to town—made the rez a prized swimming hole for boys aged 9 or so to mid-teens. The "swim suit, optional" custom offered further appeal!

The rez was also the location chosen by John Nelson to try out some samples from the large crate of fireworks he had bought in South Dakota a few days before July 4. They were not legally sold in Minnesota but were readily available across the state line a few miles west of Ruthton. As kids we tended to look upon the Dakotas as somewhat untamed, loose, and wild—the origin of our fiercest blizzards and the beginning of the West once you crossed the Missouri

River and approached the Badlands. So it seemed a logical place to get fireworks.

The fact that John, unlike most of us, could afford $60 worth of fireworks somewhat rankled in the ranks. In addition, he had a few other advantages over many of us. His parents owned the pool hall, a large building which housed a long bar, a small glass case displaying candy bars and snacks, a freezer for ice cream, booths for having drinks and snacks, four pool tables, and one or two card tables. Ruthton's only barber shop shared the front of the building, but it was a partially walled-off room with an entrance from the pool hall. Located on the floor beside that entrance was a spittoon. The barber's unstated message was: "No working the chaw while in the barber's chair." The pool hall was a center of social activity in the evenings, rivaling the bowling alley; both businesses were successful and were usually packed until late every Saturday night. John lived with his parents in an apartment above the pool hall, so he was privy to whatever was going on uptown. He also had a brother, about twelve years his senior, who was a World War II vet who gifted John with a more worldly outlook than most of us were exposed to. As we entered adolescence, John worked to familiarize himself with the minor vices of the teenage years, and he gained early success with the girls.

So, John, his pal Charlie Anderson, and a couple of other guys carried the crate of South Dakota fireworks out to the rez for a pre-Fourth of July sampler. Charlie, as it turned out, was a key member of this group, though he was just tagging along. He and John were friends from pre-school days, classmates, and football and basketball teammates, and they had spent a lot of time together just hanging out. Charlie was well liked in our group but at the same time somewhat of a loner. He was an only child, and he was painfully shy around girls throughout his high school years. It so happened that across the street from the house where he lived with his parents and grandmother there lived twin sisters of Charlie's age and of Danish ancestry. They were classic Danish beauties: tall, blond, well designed, and sure of themselves in a social setting. They seemed to enjoy Charlie's discomfort around girls, and they employed their eloquent body language to heighten his obvious unease in their presence. So, all in all, Charlie was a nice guy, a friendly guy, not an instigator, and not a trouble-maker. But shortly after the group led by John Nelson arrived at the rez, Charlie dropped a lit firecracker into the open crate! The resulting loud and lengthy detonation could be heard throughout town and beyond. Nothing of value survived. Charlie vigorously protested that it was an accident, but John never forgot, and he massaged his grudge for a long while. In the telling and retelling of this story, folks always smiled and seemed to react as though Charlie's action was not without merit. After all, it fit nicely into the community ethic of striving to keep everyone humble. Another blow against unseemly pride.

It is somewhat surprising that over the years no drownings or serious accidents occurred at the rez, at least none that any of us was aware of. This is not counting the time one year in late autumn when two of the guys, David Jackson and Robert Pike, made a raft of grain doors and poled around the rez, the water being too cold for a swim. At one point, David, about 11 years old and only a so-so swimmer, gave his pole a strong thrust and it stuck firmly in the mud. He opted to hang on to the pole rather than stay with the raft which inevitably floated away. Luckily, Robert, an excellent swimmer, jumped in after David and managed to haul him back to the raft, thus probably saving his life. For that act the local American Legion Post awarded Robert a medal at the following Memorial Day celebration.

I must confess that despite having gone out to the rez many times over the years, neither my brother nor I ever went swimming there. It was strictly forbidden by our parents, and after they explained the reason we complied. It so happened that my mother, who had five brothers and three sisters when they lived on a farm north of town on the shore of Twin Lake, told us of a family tragedy that occurred in 1911. In celebration of a special holiday in that part of Minnesota, Danish Independence Day, most folks of Danish ancestry as well as friendly sympathizers, took the day off. While the rest of the family joined the festivities in town, two of my mother's older brothers, Anker and Harry—the younger one had just turned 8—remained on the farm but set out on the lake in a flat-bottomed boat. For unknown reasons both drowned. The death certificate starkly stated: "They must have gotten into an old boat and capsized." That tragedy was subsequently referenced only with discretion in my grandparents' presence. The only times I recall it being discussed were during our annual visits to the Ruthton cemetery where we tended to the gravesites of the Park and Christensen families in preparation for the town's celebration of Decoration Day, a term that remained in effect until a formal change to Memorial Day in 1968. Those occasions provided the most opportune times for questions and discussions related to family history. Mom's simple recounting of that tragedy offered full justification for insisting that we learn to swim and obey strictures against unsupervised swimming in the rez.

Fortunately, in the years following World War II the County of Pipestone provided free swimming lessons and transportation by school bus to the large public pool in Pipestone. The bus picked up between fifteen and twenty-five of us—mostly town kids—one morning a week during a six-week stretch in summer. For about two hours we received instruction and were given free time for recreational swimming. Thanks to those lessons and frequent swimming at Twin Lake during our high school years, my friends and I became fairly good swimmers. The Pipestone pool was located in the city's large park which contained playground equipment such as swings, slides, and monkey bars and a long row of picnic tables under the trees. This was our family's favorite destination for celebrating the Fourth of July. We took advantage of the pool and all of the equipment in the park in the afternoon and then enjoyed a picnic dinner built around fried chicken, homemade baked beans, salad, dinner rolls, and homemade pie. In the years after the Pipestone Drive-In Movie Theater opened around 1947 we finished this glorious day by taking in a movie such as "Abbott and Costello Meet Frankenstein." Imagine Don and I sitting in our Chevy or Ford eating popcorn, engrossed in what we considered the comedic brilliance of Bud Abbott and Lou Costello, while our parents and grandparents sat in relative silence perhaps hoping that Don and I would be agreeable to head back home before the start of the second movie in this awesome double feature offering. Not a chance!

Ruthton Recollections

James W. Park

Connectedness—Internal and External

Ruthton's social cohesion was partly the result of its small population and the similar backgrounds shared by most of the residents. In reality we were bound together by the general realization that our economic condition depended on the health of the farm economy. And in the postwar years the farm economy did well despite the ebb and flow of commodity prices. Disputes existed between organizations representing farmers such as the Farm Bureau and Farmers' Union and between rival agricultural commodity groups such as the butter versus the oleo margarine interests. These differences were not large enough to disrupt the social tranquility even though the latter dispute involved town folks, it was long lasting, and it became entangled in state and national politics. "Oleo" was taxed heavily at the state and federal levels, and the sale of "colored" oleo was prohibited in Minnesota, well known as a dairy state, throughout this period and until 1963. The scarcity of butter during the war gave oleo a boost as did the clever practice of selling oleo in clear plastic bags that contained a dye pellet, thus evading the stricture against the sale of colored oleo. When broken in the sealed bag, the pellet containing a yellow dye, could be kneaded into the white, lard-like contents thus producing a cheaper, butter-like product. Don and I spent many hours kneading that oleo bag, and we were always fearful that the bag would rupture, though it never did.

Social cohesion was also enhanced by conscious effort. "The Ruthton Tribune," founded in 1914 by Jay and Anna Mae Jackson who served as owners/editors, writers/reporters for most of the time from then until 1950, was a critical instrument in nourishing a strong sense of community. It was a weekly newspaper filled with all of the local news that was "fit to print." During much of that time Anna Mae served as reporter, and in that capacity she visited families regularly, charmed everyone with her folksy manner, learned of family happenings, and presented the information in a conversational tone. That kind of news was eagerly consumed, and it kept readers abreast of the residents' routines, joys, and sorrows. In her reporter's capacity she frequently visited our home with notebook in hand. Jay, on the other hand, seldom entered the homes of any of the townsfolk given his crusty demeanor and his air of rugged independence. The only visit to our house I can recall was when he stopped by in his capacity as census taker in 1950. He arrived late one afternoon and asked questions about the family, the house, and its furnishings as he filled out the census form. While standing in the kitchen toward the end of his visit he asked, "What kind of refrigerator is that?" Dad answered, "It's a Kelvinator." "Gee, Floyd, sounds like a cultivator!" With that witty comment about our aging appliance and amid chuckles by all, he was out the door.

"The Ruthton Tribune" also carried a popular column, "Here and There," by Sigurd Pedersen. He had taught in the Ruthton school in the 1920s and then owned and operated a local hardware store in the 1930s. I think it was a combination of that newspaper column, his noted teaching experience, and a thoughtful manner of speaking that created an aura of learning about him. Like the Jacksons, he had deep roots in the community, and he seemed to command everyone's respect. He and his wife Edythe were active in the Danish Lutheran Church, and as a gifted vocalist she belonged to several choral groups and was a member of many social organizations. They lived in one of the largest houses in town and the only one with a garage in the basement. On those occasions when our family was invited to their home for a party, Mom admonished Don and me to be particularly mindful of our manners, because the invitees were always well behaved and rather formally dressed. In decent weather on Sunday afternoons Sigurd routinely took a brisk stroll through town wearing a suit jacket—on hot days it was seersucker. He was probably the only man in town to own such a garment. If Ruthton had a couple that was treated with some formality and as members of the elite, it was Sigurd and Edythe Pedersen.

The large number of social organizations, many of which have previously been mentioned, offered opportunities for forming friendships across ethnic and religious lines. Other occasions for get-togethers were the frequent church suppers held by the three churches in town and the Ellsborough Lutheran Church east of town. The respective Ladies Aid organizations hosted the church suppers as well as various lunches such as those offered at farm sales and auctions. Among the well-attended social gatherings were the many celebrations of twenty-fifth and fiftieth-wedding anniversaries, portions of which were usually held in the churches. A week or two prior to the anniversary date, sign-up lists were posted at the check-out counters in the grocery stores so people could donate a quarter or more toward a gift. Other opportunities for community socializing included the weekly summer-time band concerts in the park; the annual junior-class play directed by English teacher Helene Ekse in the town hall; the piano recital by students of Alice Sanderson every spring in the Norwegian Lutheran Church; the Easter cantata in the same venue also featuring Alice as organist or vocalist. Any account of the town's social events must highlight the leadership role of these women as well as those who made up the large majority of teachers in the public school, in all of the Sunday schools, and in the religious youth organizations such as the Methodist Youth Fellowship.

A well-known cliché holds that in a small town everyone knows everyone else's business. That was generally true of Ruthton. Consequently, nearly everyone's joys and misfortunes were subject to comment and analysis by the community at large. During a period of about 15 years following the mid-1950s, the town agonized over three suicides. The pain visited on the families by such trauma had to be born publicly before the entire community. Another cause of communal anguish were the town's several incidents of alcoholism. Though some of these were discretely hidden, others were on full display. The most conspicuous were the cases of two brothers who, upon returning from military service after World War II, began celebrating their survival with heavy week-end drinking bouts. The heavy drinking escalated, the men were unable to hold steady jobs, and the dysfunction in their lives remained on open display for many years. Ruthton's residents knew about and commented on most of the other cases of alcoholism even though its victims were more discrete than those two brothers. It was also quite obvious that this illness afflicted the well positioned as well as the less fortunate in the community. Another example of suffering that was quite public and much discussed was the high incidence of diabetes. The theme of much of the town's talk was the reality that a few of the victims failed to curb life-long dietary habits that proved fatal for some. The dreadful consequences in at least three cases were amputation of one or both legs and/or blindness. Ruthton's small population and its several social interconnections meant that, for good or ill, our privacy was quite limited. As an illustration, I recall several times when our family and others were guests in a particular neighbor's home where we usually sat and chatted in the living room which faced the street. Whenever someone happened to walk by outside, our host would immediately spring to his feet, go to the window, inform us who it was, and speculate about the passerby's destination and purpose. As a general rule it seemed that even the most trivial happenings could attract attention and comment.

One factor that helped Ruthton maintain itself as an interconnected community was the early creation and growth of a local telephone company. What began as the Farmer's Co-op Telephone Company in 1906 became the Ruthton Telephone Company when the former was purchased by Chris and Gladys Andersen in 1929. They expanded and modernized the phone company over the next thirty years so that when they completed the sale of their company in 1959 it was a modernized dial exchange system providing service to nearly every home and business in town and to nearby rural residents. During hard times early in the depression they relocated the switchboard from a small store on the business street into their home where they installed it in a room next to their bedroom so that Gladys, working as the primary operator, could provide service twenty-four hours a day. As the company grew she trained their five daughters to work the switchboard. The company also hired many members of the community to work as operators including my Aunt

Bernice; other employees were townspeople hired on a part-time basis to help with the varied tasks in this labor-intensive business. One was my high school friend Charlie Anderson who worked full-time for one or two summers. The work varied with the season but included repairing and installing phones, laying cables, installing and replacing lines and poles, and knocking sleet from sagging lines to keep them from breaking. I came to know Chris through his regular visits to our house to replace the batteries that powered the phone. He maintained a record of the date of each replacement so he would know when to make a return visit. Chris believed that every home should have a phone in case of emergencies such as fire, but during the 1930s some families could not afford the $1 per month telephone service rate. Consequently he came to accept goods in barter for the service—garden products, milk, eggs, chickens, and meat. Prices were also kept low by allowing rural customers to subscribe to two-, four-, or eight-party lines instead of private lines. In addition, this afforded inexpensive entertainment for some party-line subscribers. Despite his best efforts, a few families chose not to bother with a telephone. Jay and Anna Mae Jackson elected not to have a phone, so when a call came to the switchboard from their son Ben who lived out of state, one of the Andersen girls was dispatched to run over to the Jackson home, two blocks away, and fetch Anna Mae. The two then walked back to the switchboard so Anna Mae could speak with her son. That was a full-service telephone company!

Unlike the telephone which represented Ruthton's connectedness both internally and with the outside world, the rez, its associated water tower at the train depot, and the railroad tracks and crossings symbolized Ruthton's external connectedness. That symbolism remained valid even after the 1950s when diesel engines began replacing steam locomotives on Great Northern routes. Sustenance offered by the rez's waters to the thirsty, powerful locomotives had proven reliable for more than half a century. The romance of trains derived from the larger culture. That romantic attachment was strengthened by daily witnessing the passing of those conspicuous giants through Ruthton and in listening to those haunting sounds while lying in bed at night and hearing in them a summons to distant adventure. That power-in-motion beckoned young and old to come down to the depot for a close-up look. Don and I were sometimes able to persuade Dad to drive us to the depot when we were very young to witness the northbound 5 pm freight train as it roared non-stop through town while we stood transfixed on the depot platform. "Careful, don't stand too close," Dad warned as that awesome force bore down on us. The exhilaration of the thunderous roar, the warning whistle, the blast of air, the enormous power, and then the friendly wave of the proud engineer high above us lasted well beyond its disappearance over the horizon. The sensation was probably akin to the enchantment felt by the young Samuel Clemens as he watched the steamboats on the Mississippi River from the shoreline at Hannibal, Missouri.

If only we could ride the Twin Cities-bound 9 pm passenger train. Our wish was partially met one evening when the Krall boys' mom drove four or five of us kids to the depot, bought tickets, and put us on the train for a ride to Russell, a small town about twelve miles to the north. What a thrill, but, oh, so brief and hardly far enough to get up to speed! She met us with her car as promised, and all we could talk about on the drive back home was the possibility of a ride all the way to the Twin Cities. The real thing happened around 1946 when Aunt Bernice escorted Don and me on that same passenger train bound for St. Paul for a visit with our Cousin Myrna and her family. We boarded our train anticipating this adventure as an exciting introduction to the wider world, but it became a ten-hour, dusk to dawn venture in sleepless, exhausting tedium. The first hour was interesting because in the twilight we could still see the countryside and the small towns we passed through, but the next two hours brought us only as far as Willmar, a train hub about one hundred miles west of St. Paul. There we sat for at least three hours, motionless but sleepless because of the uncomfortable upright, thinly padded seats. About 3 am we resumed our plodding journey and arrived shortly after sunrise at the St. Paul depot where Uncle Howard met us three travelers, all eager for a bed and a good night's sleep. We never bragged about that trip and we never repeated it.

After a speedy recovery from our travels we spent two or three days of high adventure in St. Paul. An overflow of excitement came with our first experience using St. Paul's mass transit system of old streetcars on rails which brought us from our cousin's apartment to our downtown shopping destination in about half an hour. Upon exiting our clanging conveyance we walked to a huge department store, bought some toy soldiers for future skirmishes, huge balloons, and paddle boards with attached rubber balls. The day's climax was riding the stores moveable stairs a few times—our first experience with escalators. Luckily, Aunt Bernice purchased a photo of herself, Don, and me taken by a street photographer while we were downtown. It offers comic evidence of one young guy walking with gaze affixed upward and mouth agape, appearing as the "not-so-cool country cousin" while on his first visit to the city.

Fortunately, daily bus service to the Twin Cities and elsewhere was introduced in 1947 by Northland Greyhound, and it offered a reasonable alternative to the Great Northern Railroad's milk run.

State Senator Hans Pedersen was present for the inauguration of that service, but he did not have time to give a speech to the small group assembled—the bus had a schedule to keep, after all! In the early days of bus service the bus did not routinely stop in Ruthton, so as a signal to the driver that passengers were waiting to be picked up a red flag was hung on the light pole at the intersection of the business street and the highway. That service was offered by Clarence and Marvin Rupp, owners of Rupps' Garage located at the intersection. That bus was my chosen mode of travel for my first trip to the University of Minnesota in 1954 for freshman orientation. It was a long ride because of the many stops at large and small towns; but the trip's boredom lessened as we picked up other freshmen for the start of our common adventure.

Automobiles offered our primary connection to nearby towns and places of interest. One advantage Don and I had over most other kids in Ruthton was that we always traveled in a relatively new and well-maintained car because Dad needed a reliable vehicle for his work. Our family frequently drove to nearby towns and locales. For example, we drove to Tyler to visit friends; to Marshall for shopping; to Brookings, South Dakota to see the eye doctor; to Camden State Park for picnics; and most frequently to Pipestone for shopping, visiting relatives, hiking at the Pipestone National Monument, and attending the Song of Hiawatha Pageant or the county fair. One of our earliest, distant trips—about 150 miles—was a drive to Mitchell, South Dakota in 1946 where we joined a guided tour of the Corn Palace and then attended an evening program featuring the very popular Andrews Sisters.

By the late 1940s, improvements in both highways and cars brought comfort and reduced travel time, so our connections to our nearest large cities— Minneapolis and St. Paul and Sioux Falls, South Dakota—were becoming easier and more frequent. Travel time by car to the Twin Cities by 1950 was between four and five hours. Our family drove to St. Paul to visit Cousin Myrna's family about once every two years, and we spent two or three days with them. We made the round trip in a single day only once and never repeated it because it was too exhausting. That one time occurred when I was about 10 years old and our grandparents traveled with us. On the way back we stopped late at night for gas and a bathroom break. Walking groggily from the bathroom back toward the car, I passed a chair in the station that made me think I was home; I sat down, began getting ready for bed, took off my shoes and socks and started to undress. A bit later I heard Grandpa laughing. He helped me gather my clothes, took me by the hand, and walked me back to the car. I was indeed ready for bed! The drive to Sioux Falls, on the other hand, was only about 90 minutes, and we drove there about once a year. That was also my mother's destination when she and her two best friends, Alice Sanderson and Marie Jagt, took the better part of a day once a year to escape for shopping, dining, and catching up. When Mom returned home usually around 6 or 7 pm, Grandma would be downstairs waiting impatiently while peering out the windows, and as soon as the door opened Grandma would utter the strongest admonition I ever heard from her, "Poor Floyd and the boys. Supper time, and no supper." Mom would smile and reply, "It's a good thing the fridge is full of food."

Our most memorable family vacation was a six-week trip we took in 1948 driving throughout the West including California and Oregon. We spent about four weeks staying with relatives and friends on the West coast beginning in San Diego and working our way northward to Bend, Oregon. For Don and me this was a remarkable adventure that gave us an advantage over most other kids in Ruthton. Five years later we repeated it but with a few variations. By my senior year in high school I considered myself well travelled and "connected," though I had never been east of the Mississippi River, that is, with the exception of several visits to St. Paul.

The lure of the West, and especially of California, was powerful when growing up. Its strong attraction had many sources such as its varied natural beauty—mountains, deserts, and ocean beaches; the romanticism of Hollywood; the exotic names such as San Juan Capistrano or Rancho Cucamonga, a delightful name for a city southeast of Los Angeles popularized by Jack Benny on his radio program; locations such as Death Valley, Alcatraz, Yosemite, and the Golden Gate Bridge; and family stories from the 1930s of drinking all the fresh orange juice you wanted for 10 cents. But the most powerful lure came from the burgeoning defense industry of Southern California beginning in 1941 and continuing through the war years. Some prominent families in Ruthton were part of that exodus: Walter and Ida Svenning, my friend David Svenning's parents; Art and Ruth Jones, active members of the Methodist Church. Ruth was one of Mom's closest friends, and their younger daughter, Roberta, was my age and a girl I had a crush on. Another prominent family that followed their adult daughter to California in 1946, Harry and Carrie Madsen, were the owners of Madsen's grocery store. In addition, some of Ruthton's young men who enlisted for military service traveled to California for training or for temporary assignments. Some yielded to its lure in the postwar years. My Uncle Ben, Mom's younger brother, told of enlisting in the army in Minnesota, boarding the troop train in mid-winter, arriving in Los Angeles, and after getting off the train feeling that something was amiss as he looked up at the palm trees while still wearing his Minnesota long-johns. He ultimately settled in the greater Los Angeles area.

Other connections to the world outside of Ruthton were vital to our citizenship and to our sense of place in the country and in the world. Newsreels, newspapers, and radio kept us abreast of current events. The newsreels shown before every movie at the Rex Theater were often dramatic and memorable. An example is film of the invasion of France in World War II which began with the Normandy landings on June 6, 1944. Another is newsreels showing the solemn movement of the train conveying the body of the suddenly deceased President Franklin D. Roosevelt from Warm Springs, Georgia to Washington, D. C. Despite the emotional impact of such newsreels, they may have had limited influence because they were seen irregularly and by only a select, movie-going part of the population. The morning and evening newspapers published in Minneapolis and delivered daily were read by probably no more than forty percent of the town's residents. Those of us who worked as paperboys had a good sense of our clients from collecting for the week's subscription every Saturday, and that experience showed that the number of customers varied only slightly over time, and that they represented less than half the population.

Most influential in dissemination of the news was the radio, and it remained dominant from the 1930s until the late 1950s. A reasonable estimate is that at least ninety percent of Ruthton's households owned a radio by the early 1940s. Even the poorest families had one—you could hear it playing inside a home as you rode by on your bike. The Jacksons, who lacked most modern conveniences, had a radio. Whenever I happened to be with David in their house late in the afternoon, I often heard Anna Mae listening to her favorite radio programs, "Lum and Abner"—a popular spoof of hillbilly life that had a long run (1931-1954)—and a folksy musical program hosted by Burl Ives whose signature song, "Jimmy Crack Corn," made no sense to me. In our house in a living room corner we had a large radio in a four-foot tall wooden console, and my grandparents had their own console upstairs. To service and repair these many radios in the Ruthton area, we had a small repair shop housed in an office in the John Deere Implement dealership. In the immediate postwar period portable radios—about the size of a lunch pail or a tackle box—became popular. In our house it sat on the kitchen counter so we could listen to the news while having breakfast or lunch. After the lunch-time news Don and I joined Mom in listening to her favorite soap opera, "Ma Perkins." At supper time when Dad ate with us, the radio remained silent, so we spent that time eating and talking to each other.

One of the frustrations facing radio listeners was the occasional poor quality of reception. The problem was acute whenever there was a thunderstorm in the vicinity. Even absent such atmospheric disturbances, reception could be compromised by unknown sources, what folks referred to as "electricity in the air." To enhance our radio reception from the several stations broadcasting out of Minneapolis and Sioux Falls, Dad installed a long, wire antenna from the roof to a large tree. That improved matters but didn't solve the problem. In fact the quality of reception was influenced by factors largely beyond our control— distance, weather, and geography. An example of the role of geography occurred during our trip out West in 1948. During our visit with Uncle Bill and Aunt Alice in Stockton, California, Dad and Uncle Bill were eager to listen to a much-anticipated heavyweight boxing match broadcast from Yankee Stadium. Bill knew that we would not be able to get decent reception in Stockton, so he proudly invited us into his new Nash and he drove us into the mountains east of the city where we listened to it on his car radio. This was the famous match featuring Joe Louis toward the end of his boxing career and Jersey Joe Walcott, a rematch of the previous year's split decision that went to Louis. He won the 1948 fight with a knockout in the eleventh round, and I believe we were all pleased with the outcome. He had had a brilliant career in the 1930s, enlisted in the army shortly after we entered the war, and used his fame to promote the sale of war bonds. His achievements came despite being victimized by what we later learned was a pattern of ugly racial discrimination.

The dominance of radios as our prime news source and as a major source of entertainment was coming to an end by the late 1950s because of the arrival of TV and of its much improved reception. There can be no question that by 1960 we were more thoroughly connected to life outside of Ruthton than ever before. The thirst for more complete and more current information grew as the pace of change seemed to quicken. There may have been unease at the rate of change, but we had little sense of the impending chaos of the 1960s.

Work, Responsibility, and Pride

As I moved through elementary school and into junior high school I held some small jobs that boys my age were taking on, such as mowing lawns, shoveling snow, delivering a daily newspaper, and working as a janitor. One of those janitorial jobs involved making sure that the meeting place upstairs above the Red Owl Store was swept, dusted, and generally set in good order. It was used by several organizations including the Eastern Star, Masons, Royal Neighbors, and American Legion. It was easy work because most of those groups were neat and orderly with the notable exception of the American Legion—boy, did those guys know how to party! Some jobs were arranged by my mother who was very ambitious for Don and me. She saw this work commitment as a way to keep us out of trouble and point us in the right direction—to start thinking about going to college and saving money for it.

My brother and I grew up intuitively knowing we would go to college after high school. My mother's message to me was rather specific but not insistent: go to a public two-year business school in Minnesota and follow the path of Uncle Holger—her older brother— to become a successful businessman. When I cautiously pushed back and expressed a preference for the University of Minnesota, she offered little encouragement. Dad was silent on the subject. He had attended Hamline University in St. Paul for one or two quarters, and it was not a positive experience. A part-time job he had counted on failed to materialize, and as an entering freshman he felt demeaned by treatment received from upperclassmen and from a particular geography professor. It also turned out that he could not continue the physics class he had registered for because he lacked a critical prerequisite. This information about Dad's college experience is something he never freely talked about. Don and I had to vigorously extract it from him, and in this we were aided by Mom's gentle nudging. He had attended high school in Pipestone, and had, in fact, received a secondary education superior to mine, particularly in foreign language and mathematics. In advising me, my mother may have feared a repeat of Dad's disappointment at Hamline.

Her ambition for us boys was probably motivated by the economic pain her parents had endured during the depression years when they lost their farm and by its impact on her life. When she finished Mankato State Teachers College in 1927, she found a one-year teaching position in a small town north of the Twin Cities. Shortly thereafter, her parents asked her to help them out by returning home and applying for a local teaching job. She made the move, found such a position in a country school, and bought a car. A year later she landed a job teaching grade six in the Ruthton Public School. That year, 1929, also marked the passing of Alvin, her very talented 19-year old younger brother. His death certificate declared that the cause of death was heart trouble and bronchitis, and it included the statement: "He was in delicate health since childhood." Though she answered the family's request for help, her assistance only slowed the irreversible slide toward bankruptcy which was triggered by substantial medical bills, drought conditions, the depression, and the poorer quality of the land on the new farm they had moved to in order to be closer to town and to the school. This family misfortune, however, contained a silver lining in that within two years of her return she became better acquainted with our dad when he had the good fortune to be able to help her out one day when she was stranded with a car problem.

Another reason Mom encouraged Don and me to think seriously about formal education beyond high school was the very personal example of her own family. She and Holger, the two oldest siblings, obtained their post-secondary education and had done well. In contrast, the two youngest siblings, Aunt Bernice and Uncle Ben, finished high school in the midst of the Great Depression, did not go beyond that level, and they subsequently struggled. When Ben returned from World War II, Mom strongly encouraged him to use the generous benefits of the GI Bill to advance his education, either in an academic or vocational field. The hard times of the 1930s no longer offered a valid excuse, and yet he would have none of it. She always treated him with family affection and generosity, but she was certainly frustrated by his stubbornness on the subject

That tension between them had existed for many years, and I suspect that one of the early events that nurtured it occurred when I was about two years old, and we all lived on the farm. One of my few memories from that time was of a summer morning when I decided to walk to the barn to watch Grandpa and Uncle Ben milk the cows. As they were sitting on their milk stools, Ben asked me if I could help by holding the cow's tail so it wouldn't swing in his face as he was milking. Then I heard, "Hold on real tight with both hands." I was happy to be included as part of the milking party, so I did my duty and firmly gasped it. In short order the cow swished her tail, I held on, lost my balance, and fell on my back into the soggy, stinking, fresh manure in the gutter. I immediately began crying, slowly raised myself from the muck, and stiffly made my way toward the house. My mother and grandmother were outside hanging up the laundry, and as I approached them I could hear Uncle Ben laughing above the sound of my bawling. I remember Mom glared at him, fetched a pail of water and began working on the reeking mess standing before her. I can only guess at the message she imparted to Ben when she finished the task at hand.

By the time I entered high school I had become the church pianist and accepted a role in working with its choir. I had taken piano les-

Life on the Farm

sons for many years from Mom's close friend, Alice Sanderson, and I practiced a lot. Despite receiving generous compliments I gradually came to realize that, though competent, I was not musically gifted— certainly less so than my brother. This enlightenment came through a minor incident I refer to as "The Day Ramsted Came to Town." Ramsted was a musicologist and a much -esteemed friend of my piano teacher. Her description of him led me to think of him as ranking somewhere up there with the famed conductor, Arturo Toscanini. Ramsted arrived for one of his periodic visits with her family just in time for the spring piano recital of 1953 which he planned to attend. I remember him as an elderly, tall, slender man dressed in a suit, vest, and tie who presented the aspect of a humorless parson. He was not very social; in fact, my teacher explained that instead of sitting in the auditorium during the recital, he preferred to remain alone in his car, parked near the building's open windows. Following the recital, which I thought went well, Ramsted spoke to me privately. The essence of his solemn message was that I was pretty good technically, but that I had no feeling for the music or connection with it. I accepted his message with good grace which was not difficult because it was delivered thoughtfully, and I felt there was some merit to it. In hindsight, his observations may have planted a seed that, if nourished, could—at the right time—offer a rationale for cutting back on practice time and gaining some freedom from a full schedule.

Shortly before this, our church was considering buying an electric organ to supplement the piano. A committee was formed with two musicians on it—the high school music teacher and my piano teacher—plus three church members including myself. I was committed to learning to play the organ if the purchase was made, and I felt rather exalted to be serving on this committee which was charged with assisting in fund raising and making a recommendation to the Church Board as to the preferred brand and model of organ. The process lasted several weeks and involved visiting dealerships and locations where different organs were in use. Prior to our committee's decision a well-known church member with strong feelings on the subject approached the Board with a proposed solution. This parishioner had recently made a good profit from a cattle sale, and he offered to pay for the instrument with the proviso that his preference get the nod. This was the same Board that would not buy a

TV antenna for our poet-minister and the same generous man who again came to the rescue, Morris Minett. The process was thus taken out of our hands. The Board made an easy decision, the committee was disbanded with thanks for its service, and I began taking organ lessons on the instrument I had not favored.

Within a few days of that action, the Easter cantata singers held one of their regular practices at the Norwegian Lutheran Church after which we all adjourned for coffee, punch, cookies, and socializing in the church basement. During a pause in the conversation, one of the singers, Nels Nelson, asked me about the work of the Methodist organ committee. I welcomed this as an opportunity to shine, to describe the process we had gone through, the places visited, the discussions we had held, and the difficulty of our decision. In short, I was eloquent in describing the process and its importance. When I finished, Nels calmly observed, "I understand that Morris's cattle helped you with your difficult decision." He delivered that observation with deftness and with a slight smile. How could I have forgotten that Ruthton held few secrets and of how quickly news traveled? In many ways, Nels was the perfect messenger for this gentle chiding. He was a soft-spoken, kindly, respected businessman—owner of a farm-implement dealership—and a prominent member of the Norwegian Lutheran Church and of the community at large. Nels was an effective watchdog in the ongoing struggle against unseemly pride!

James W. Park

The Town Hall

By the mid-1950s tangible signs of Ruthton's material progress were evident. The most notable signs included purchase of two new fire engines and construction of a new fire station, a new post office, and a large addition to the school including an expansive auditorium. The fire house was located in midtown, and fire protection was provided by volunteers. Until the purchase of those new fire engines, the town and surrounding farms relied on a fire engine mounted on a 1928 Chevrolet truck chassis, and the whole contraption turned out to be not so reliable in its later years. Notice of a fire came through the frightening sound of the town's siren, the same startling sound that daily announced high noon. Two blasts from the siren signaled a fire in town and three meant in the country—or maybe it was the other way around. We kids as well as many adults could never keep it straight, evidence that fires were infrequent. It didn't really matter because we all headed to the fire station by car, bike, or afoot to learn of the fire's location. The first task was to assemble the volunteers and get the fire engine started. Occasionally it would not start, and it had to be towed. If it was not a school day we kids would mount-up on our bikes and become part of the parade even into the country if the distance were less than three miles or so. Like train derailments, heavy blizzards, and farm accidents, fires were rare, disruptive of our routines, and sometimes spectacular.

The most consequential local fire for me, though easily contained and of little danger to anyone, occurred late on Halloween night, 1948. Dad had awakened us as soon as he realized that an unusual, bright light engulfing our house was coming from Jay Jackson's backyard barn going up in flames. As the light from the midnight conflagration illuminated our faces, our expressions surely reflected the shock we all felt and the frustration of the compelled passivity of mere observers. There we stood, the four of us in our pajamas—Dad, Mom, Don, and me—staring eastward out of our kitchen windows at the blaze only half a block away. Neither villain nor cause was ever identified. The Jacksons had no enemies, and the barn had no electrical wiring. But it was an old structure with mangers and an upstairs haymow, and it contained combustible material such as wood and cardboard. A Halloween "trick" was hardly plausible in a town where the most audacious act of vandalism was toppling outhouses. But Jacksons' outhouse remained upright even though it was located next to the barn, and it was an inviting target for pranksters because it was one of the few in town still in daily use. The town's firemen arrived in time to prevent the fire from totally consuming the structure, though it was nevertheless a total loss. They extinguished it primarily to save Svennings' barn just across the alley and some large, nearby maple trees.

In our family I was the most grief-stricken because for years that barn had been one of my favorite haunts. It's the place where many of us kids, aged six to our early teens, gathered to make sling-shots, build bird houses, work on our bikes, do target practice with our

Red Ryder BB guns, and tinker with a small gasoline engine David had acquired a few weeks before the fire. The benefit from all of that fooling around was that we learned how to use a variety of hand tools, and David had quite an assortment. Learning handicraft skills was fundamental to life in Ruthton where basic knowledge of carpentry, painting, and plumbing was assumed. Incidentally, the upstairs haymow where no adult ever ventured—the steep climb was too difficult for David's grandparents—was our special place where we could experiment with cigarettes or carefully examine and discuss the forbidden photos borrowed or secreted from any of our older, experienced brothers, especially those who were returning vets.

To make room for Ruthton's new post office, a large wooden structure commonly referred to as the "town hall" or in earlier decades as the "opera house," was demolished. That building, put up in the 1890s at the eastern end of what became the business street, had served as a gathering place for various town activities, and it remained functional until shortly before it was torn down. That old building housed lots of memories, including my mother's memories of where she learned to play basketball. The town hall was a cavernous building with a basement for storing things such as large numbers of wooden folding chairs, a stage with curtain and confined dressing area behind it, and a small balcony which offered prized seating for crowded events. In winter it was used for roller skating on Saturday afternoons when skates were handed out free of charge by Henry Huhnstock in his roles as town sheriff and manager of infrastructure. It was also used during basketball season for practice by the high school team and for some school P. E. classes—it was only a block from the school. In the late 1940s the town hall served as the venue for celebrating the fiftieth-wedding anniversary of Jay and Anna Mae Jackson. The master of ceremonies at that festive event was State Senator Hans Pedersen who introduced the couple and advised the packed house that the Jacksons were a bit tardy in arriving because Jay had had to wait for his wife who was always slow in getting dressed because "she had to slow down for the curves." To my youthful ears that passed as very clever humor from our distinguished Senator!

For many years the American Legion Post used the town hall on the week-end before Thanksgiving to hold what was called "a turkey shoot." It offered an opportunity to earn a duck, goose, or turkey by winning at a game of chance—cards, dice, or bingo. When I was about 10 years old I won a duck by playing bingo. I could hardly believe such good luck at what was my first experience at the annual turkey shoot. The live birds were in crates stacked on the stage, and in claiming my duck the poultry attendant in charge, Bill North, carefully showed me how to hold and carry the bird so it would not escape. He also warned, "Even if the duck decides to poop on that nice winter coat, don't let go!" Naturally, in this farm community no one saw any need to provide a cardboard box or a gunny sack for carrying the live prize, so I tucked him under my right arm and firmly held his neck in my left hand as instructed. My duck and I arrived home without incident and without a single quack. I walked triumphantly into our living room and proudly introduced Mom to my prize. She was not thrilled with this nervous-looking bird in her very neat and clean living room, but she assured me that the duck would become part of our holiday dinner. I then took my new friend—he had caused no difficulties—down the basement and put him under a large box for safe keeping. Mom promised that Grandpa would know what to do in the morning. As it turned out, he not only knew what to do, he seemed to enjoy it.

Bill North, that poultry attendant who was so concerned about my winter coat, was a young man I had known for many years. He was an older brother of a friend and classmate, David North, and he was a full-time employee at Bill Popp's Produce and Hatchery. A few years before that town hall incident with the duck, my mother had assigned me with what became a periodic task of walking the two blocks to Bill Popp's carrying a pail and buying "a three or four pound springer"—not a rooster or a laying hen but a tender young chicken. Bill North always waited on me, and with pleasure he would tell me to bring my pail and follow him as he grabbed a springer from one of the many stacked crates. We then walked back to an open area behind Popp's Produce. With a wry smile he advised me to stand back and watch carefully as he took the bird by the head, swung it in a full circle a few times, and then released the body while holding the severed head. The springer then did a frenzied death dance and finally fell into a quivering pile of feathers at which point Bill picked it up and deposited it in my pail. Thereby I gained a vivid understanding of the expression, "He ran around like a chicken with his head cut off."

My warmest memories of our town hall are linked to the performances there of the junior-class plays presented every fall. Helene Ekse, the long-standing high school English teacher and school librarian, was the drama coach and was in full charge of the entire production including sets, lighting, and costumes. Mrs. Ekse, a graduate of Minnesota's highly prestigious Carleton College, set high standards in her classes and brought enthusiasm, humor, and polish to whatever she undertook. In 1953 my junior class presented a three-act farce, "The Mummy and the Mumps," and more than half the class had roles on stage and off. Preparations went on for weeks and involved multiple evening rehearsals. I had a role in the play doing two things I had never done before—singing a solo in public without accompaniment and kissing a girl in public. For the former, Mrs. Ekse advised me to choose any popular song that was showy but not difficult. I chose "When Irish Eyes Are Smiling"— easy, tuneful, and with memorable lyrics —but I refused to sing it until the final dress rehearsal because of shyness. The second task offered an even greater challenge to my shyness. However, my partner was Darlene Evink, a comely red-head with a winning smile, an attractive figure, and beautiful singing voice. She and I had become good friends as classmates and through a shared membership in our high school octet. She also had a long-term boyfriend, an older guy from a neighboring town. As in the case of public singing I informed Mrs. Ekse that I would not kiss Darlene until the final dress rehearsal. The drama coach qui-

etly suggested some private practice might ease the tension, but then there was the matter of that boyfriend. On the night of dress rehearsal the singing part went well, and to my great delight the kissing part was wonderful! Despite some nervousness, Darlene was very cooperative, she smelled so good, and she was so soft! By the end of our second performance on stage before the town's multitudes, I had fit comfortably into my, oh, so envied role.

Helene Ekse, English Teacher and Drama Coach, 1953

Heavy Labor

When considering the lifestyle of people of my parents' and grandparents' generations, the toll imposed by prolonged, heavy labor is striking. Prior to today's mechanization of heavy farm work, a lifetime of farming often led to physical breakdown. Though some farmers were able to retire early and move into town, most felt compelled to continue working, and as a group they did not offer an enviable image of comfortable aging. At the same time, many accepted their fate with good humor. This was true of my grandfather, possibly because bankruptcy had forced him into an early retirement which allowed him to escape the debilitation suffered by some of his friends. He sometimes helped farmer friends at critical times such as fall harvest. One year in the late 1940s he was helping make silage on a farm owned by Carl Madsen—one of those friends, a fellow Dane, and a member Grandpa's church. At one point late in the work day the auger jammed, and he impatiently kicked the corn stalks in with his foot. The auger grabbed his pants leg and started to pull his leg into the shredder, but the operator managed to stop it before it mangled his foot and leg. He ended up with lots of bruises and cuts, refused to go to the doctor, and suffered no lasting injury. The next day Carl and his wife Johanna came calling and presented Grandpa with a new pair of overalls, declaring, "Well, it's the right thing to do." My grandfather expressed his gratitude and joked about the near disaster.

Grave and sometimes fatal farm accidents also occurred. An interesting case was that of Anton "Swede" Nelson, a bachelor farmer who lived on a small farm about two miles out of town. Anton was a stereotypical bachelor with few graces; dressing up for church meant wearing a rumpled black suit of 1920s vintage. But he was a good man and a hard worker. One day his neighbor, Obert Udstuen—my friend Robert's dad—noticed the lack of normal activity at Anton's place, so he drove over and found Anton lying on the ground badly injured and unable to move. Two days earlier his tractor had overturned and left him helpless with badly broken legs; but his immediate complaint focused on his chickens, relentlessly trying to peck at his face. He was transported to the hospital, had a full but long recovery, and was the subject of regional newspaper accounts of his ordeal. These stories caught the attention of an enterprising widow in South Dakota who paid him a visit in the hospital and then another and then began a campaign which we rather impolitely called a "courtship" that led in short order to their marriage.

The railroad maintenance crew—about five or six in all—represented another group of Ruthton men engaged in heavy manual labor. They lived by working with pick ax, shovel, and sledge hammer and were responsible for the repair and upgrade of the train tracks in all kinds of weather. As a group they had a more severely weather-beaten look than any others in town, and they all seemed advanced in years. I can think of no young men who ever sought to join their ranks. The challenges and responsibilities of their work were emphasized by an eighteen-car derailment of a freight train that took place in the mid-1940s about two miles southwest of town. Because the accident site was close to the highway, large crowds gathered for several days to watch the clean-up process and speculate about the cause of the derailment which was undetermined. The derailed cars had been loaded with a variety of freight which was largely undamaged and salvaged.

Labor, But Not Too Heavy

By the time I was in the eighth grade I was able to get a job as a stock clerk in Johnson's Fairway Grocery Store. The owners, Mel and Evelyn Johnson, employed five full-time workers and about three part-timers. From that time until I left for college, I worked about twenty to twenty-five hours a week during the school year, including a 7 am to 10 pm Saturday schedule, and full-time in the summer. This job enabled me to give up all of the small jobs that had kept me busy. It was part of a pattern in which boys my age took similar summer and after-school jobs in the local businesses. The following examples suggest other available options: work with Andrew Beck to harvest ice at Twin Lake, haul it into town, and bury it under mounds of sawdust in his ice house; work with Walter and Eldon Orange in the many bee yards located on farms in the surrounding countryside and extract honey in the bee barn; help Chris Andersen string telephone line and repair phones; work at the grain elevator to unload and store corn, soybeans, and grain delivered from the farms and later load it onto railroad cars for shipment; work in the creamery to process milk into butter; pump gas at a filling station; set pins in the bowling alley; sell tickets at the movie theater; deliver milk for Tom Scotting's dairy;

work with a plumber, carpenter, or painter; shovel chicken manure out of Art Beck's hen house. Quite a variety of jobs and some a bit more pleasant and with greater potential than others.

Johnson's Store was a successful business, though it faced competition from a traditional rival, the Red Owl Store—successor to Madsen's Store—and from a growing threat, the exciting, new "supermarket" in Pipestone, less than twenty miles distant. Customer loyalty was one factor cultivated by the owner to maintain a competitive edge. In selecting the staff of about eight, Mel kept a judicious eye toward an appeal to ethnic/religious loyalties. Employee identities included Danes, Norwegians, Dutch, Irish-Catholic, Methodists, and, for good measure, the religiously non-affiliated. It worked because these identities, by and large, were often celebrated with good humor and not with bitter rivalries or hatreds. Robert Udstuen, one of my classmates for all of our twelve years of school, loved to observe, as a proud son of a son of Norway—at the appropriate moment: "Ten thousand Swedes went through the weeds, chased by one Norwegian!" And this usually drew chuckles from all.

My closest coworker in the grocery store was Jimmy Burns, a boy one year older than I. When I arrived he had been working there about a year and knew the ropes, so I followed his lead. Jimmy was an Irish lad distinguished by his smiling, freckled face, curly hair, slender but athletic build, and a winning personality. Everyone liked him, and he loved to talk and spend time with the customers. His skill in charming the girls was a marvel which I envied. Jimmy and his younger sister lived with their mother who was a long-term first-grade teacher who commanded everyone's respect in Ruthton. They were one of a handful of Catholic families in town, and they attended church regularly. While at work Jimmy shared his thoughts about different girls, identified specific targets and goals, and shared more information with me than he should have. But I could hardly pretend I wasn't interested. His principal target for dating during that first year we worked together was Frances Erickson, a beautiful, petite, dark-haired girl with a delightful smile. At the time, the fall of 1951, when Jimmy's ambition was most ardent, she was elected homecoming queen, and this entitled the football captain, my neighbor Duane Nelsen, to crown her during the football game's halftime ceremony and give her a kiss in the presence of her four attendants and a large crowd gathered on the sidelines. What anticipation as the towering gridiron captain approached the demure queen! Duane was six feet tall, handsome, muscular, athletic, and in full football gear minus the helmet when he planted the kiss. And what a kiss—full-mouth, prolonged, and sustained by a football player's firm embrace. Her discomfort was obvious, but Duane acted as though it was all just for fun. Subsequent to "the kiss," Jimmy's expressed interest in Frances quickly dwindled. Why this loss of interest I could not explain, but shortly thereafter he directed his focus to another very attractive girl, one who lived in town. The reality facing Jimmy was that Frances was a faithful Lutheran who lived with her extended family on a farm several miles east of town and that within a few months she would graduate and be off to college. After graduating from Augustana College in Sioux Falls, Frances married a Lutheran minister.

At Johnson's Store while Jimmy was taking time from work to chat with the customers, I attempted to emulate his sociability by joining the conversations. We were spending so much time chit-chatting that our assigned duties lagged behind Mel's reasonable expectations. Mel suggested that something had to change, and with no meaningful response from us he assigned some of our responsibilities to the full-time employees. But still we made no significant changes, though I felt increasingly caught between pleasing Jimmy by consciously not outperforming him or pleasing my boss by focusing on the job. Finally, Mel offered a painful assessment of how the pair of us together stacked up against a sole, prior stock clerk, Chuck Erlandson, whom everyone admired. I took the hint—actually, it was a mandate—made a choice in favor of our very patient boss and began to do all of the work the two of us were supposed to do. And I discovered the pleasure that comes from pride of work. Within six months Jimmy announced he was leaving the job because it didn't give him enough time for school and sports. And he was an outstanding athlete. We never had an argument about work, and we remained friends through the rest of our high school years. I think we both felt we had each made the right decision—I about learning the job and doing it well and Jimmy about getting out of the stock-clerking business.

My remaining four years of work at the store were rewarding. I gained in confidence as my performance improved, and Mel gave me additional responsibilities. I thoroughly enjoyed my job, though not enough to follow Mom's suggestion: after high school go for a two-year business degree so you will be prepared to become manager of a supermarket, a much admired achievement of a family friend, Earl Madsen, who was manager of the largest supermarket in Mankato. Among my varied duties, aside from the basic tasks of stocking shelves and waiting on customers at the meat counter and checkout counter, I candled eggs purchased directly from farmers, helped take the annual inventory of all merchandise, delivered groceries to the house-bound in Mel's old jalopy, and fetched and sold lutefisk from the smelly wooden casks of lye water in which it was stored. One of the great advantages of this job was that it allowed me to become acquainted with folks I would not normally have gotten to know, particularly the many farmers who shopped regularly in the store. Indeed there was an interesting party of three who shopped in Ruthton not more than once or twice a year, but who really stocked up on those rare occasions. They were somewhat elderly, rustic-looking folks, shabbily dressed but carrying plenty of cash. The party consisted of two men, possibly brothers, plus someone they referred to as their housekeeper, Susie, who was missing several teeth. No one in town seemed to know much about them, but they claimed to live somewhere "way out in the country, west of town." I remember them also because Mel asked the clerks to keep a discrete eye on them because he feared that, while shopping, an item might per chance make it into one of their pockets instead of into the shopping cart. But no such thing happened during my tenure. In their very humble appearance and comportment they reminded me of Whistling John from an earlier time.

Although Melvin Johnson was officially listed as the proprietor of Johnson's Fairway Store, his wife Evelyn served as a strong partner in running the business. In fact she was in charge of operating the dry goods section which sold work clothes—overalls, pants, shirts, and jackets plus work shoes and boots—in addition to cloth by the yard and all manner of sewing material. They each had distinct areas of responsibility, and they often worked side-by-side, especially during those long fifteen-hour workdays every Saturday. They formed a good partnership, complemented each other's strengths and weaknesses, and were patient and considerate in their treatment of employees. Evelyn remained cheerful and never appeared overburdened despite a crowded schedule that included bringing up two daughters, help-ing her aging parents live independently in their home in town, and remaining active in several social organizations. She was an effective problem-solver and an astute businesswoman as shown in her pur-chases of merchandise for sale in the dry goods section.

The Johnsons are but one example of nine or ten cases of married couples who successfully managed businesses in Ruthton. One that merits further comment is the Red Owl Grocery Store opened by Harold and Agnes Larson about 1950. Until then Harold had made a living driving a gravel truck and Agnes had worked for many years as a waitress in a local restaurant. They pooled their savings, bought the former Madsen's Store after Chris Madsen passed away, and substantially remodeled the store giving it an appealing up-to-date look. In the process they converted the second floor from a meeting hall—the one I had serviced as janitor in earlier days—to their own apartment. They hired town residents to staff the business including my friend, Ron Krall, two years younger than I. They spent most hours of every workday managing the business in what appeared to be an equitable division of labor and responsibility. Their success during the next several years offered a conspicuous example of upward mobility through hard work and entrepreneurship. In remodeling the store they left intact a set of sturdy, metal hitching posts located on the west side of the store. This proved fortunate because on at least two occasions those hitching posts were put to good use by a farmer or two with a sleigh and a team of horses following an unusually strong blizzard which left the roads otherwise impassible. Indeed, into the 1950s a few farmers such as Pete Frederickson who had a small plot of land with garden, pasture, and barn just north of town still kept horses—maybe for nostalgia or, as they would say, "For just such an emergency, because you never know!"

One summer afternoon when working in Johnson's Store I noticed when looking out the back window, Evelyn and Agnes were walking together on their way back to work at their respective grocery stores. They were engaged in conversation while returning from a gathering of the Ruthton Women's Club. I had never had much personal contact with Agnes, but like all of the town's residents we knew of each other. I knew she was hard working, but I considered her a bit loud and course, that is, for a woman. Later that afternoon at work I commented to Evelyn that I had noticed her walking with Agnes and then I added the gratuitous remark that in my mind Agnes was kind of brash and crude. My only explanation of such an observation was that I was probably trying to curry favor with my boss by uttering that dig at her competitor. Evelyn was silent for a moment, then she looked directly at me and said, "I'm sorry to hear you say that, James, especially after the complimentary things she said about you." I was stunned and speechless. Sixty-plus years later I retain a vivid recollection of that much-deserved admonition from someone I respected.

While I was learning the job in Johnson's Store, other boys about my age were taking jobs in the town's various businesses. One example was Robert Pike, the boy who had rescued David Jackson at the rez. The first entry on Robert's resume was delivering a daily newspaper, and it was Robert who introduced me to the paper route and trained me as his successor on the morning route. At the same time he also worked on an "as needed" basis at the Phillips 66 filling station and on a fixed schedule in the drug store behind the soda fountain and in helping the pharmacist. In 1950 when the newly-assigned Methodist minister and his wife arrived, their first stop was at the Phillips 66 station where Robert pumped gas for them. Later in the day they went to the drug store for some medication where Robert waited on them, and when the Minneapolis paper was delivered that evening, Robert was the paper boy. They subsequently noted that their initial impression of Ruthton was of a town that could be run by a teenager. If the minister had ever visited the school he might have been shocked to observe Robert working as the grading assistant to the junior high school's most demanding teacher, Howard Olson. In addition to being very competent but modest, Robert was seen as trustworthy and discrete. He may have known everything going on in town, but he kept it to himself.

My best friend through elementary school was David Jackson, a boy who kept just as busy as Robert, and who was that near-drowning victim at the rez. David lived with and was raised by his paternal grandparents, Jay and Anna Mae Jackson. The Jacksons were a remarkable couple for their marked literacy and intelligence, their wide-ranging experiences such as prospecting for gold, traveling throughout the West, and gathering Native American artifacts to form a large, museum-worthy collection. Jay Jackson possessed the aura of a man of the West. He still owned his prospector's pick; some of us kids knew that he kept a six-shooter with holster and ammo, and townspeople knew that the couple had spent time in the mid-1920s in Arizona where Jay searched for the Lost Dutchman Gold Mine. The Jacksons also offered a distinctive appearance—she always wore a full-length dress while he always sported a ten-gallon hat and a brown suit with vest and tie. Before settling in Ruthton they had made a living in their travels by providing custom printing services out of their print shop on wheels. Upon their arrival in 1914 they started publishing the weekly "Ruthton Tribune" with Jay as editor and printer and Anna Mae as reporter. She was also knowledgeable on a variety of topics; in fact, she taught my mother the secrets of successful canning of fruits and vegetables. Anna Mae was a noted gardener and Jay was a skilled fisherman. He loved the sport but did not have a reliable car which was needed to drive to the area's best lake for serious fishing, Lake Shetek. It was a large, deep, beautiful lake with islands, docks, and campsites about 25 miles southeast of town. Occasionally in the summer John Huhnstock drove Jay and

David to Lake Shetek and left them for two or three days of camping and fishing, and at the end of that time he drove over and picked them up. The Jacksons also drew attention by their occasional spirited arguments. Despite their many positive qualities, the task of raising a boy was a daunting challenge because they lacked the energy of a young couple, and they lived on a very limited budget in a house that lacked a telephone, plumbing, insulation, and heating except for a pot-bellied stove in their living room. But they succeeded in their parenting task to a remarkable degree because they had lots of help from the village of Ruthton.

Jackson's Print Shop

David had an aptitude for and a keen interest in things mechanical, and he was mentored by several people who knew their crafts: auto mechanics, carpenters, gas station owners, and general handymen. An early indicator of his talents came when, at about the age of twelve, he negotiated the purchase of a Model T Ford from a long-retired painter we all knew only as "Deaf-Andrew." Actually this Model T was one of three he purchased as a kid; the first one he bought for $8 and made a good profit, selling it for $12. The Deaf-Andrew car had not been moved in many years, but with lots of help from his young friends David managed to get it pushed down the street a couple of blocks to his backyard where for many months he and his friends—including myself as an eager apprentice—tinkered, tuned up, and generally fooled around with it until we got it running. About a year later the large backyard barn that he used for his workshop burned to the ground destroying all of his tools. Townspeople generously responded to a fund-raising effort that led to collection of enough money to buy new tools and replace the barn with a smaller shed which served the purpose well. By the time David entered junior high school he had acquired an easy familiarity with things mechanical, and that enabled him to land a job in the town's principal hardware store, the Gamble Store.

The shed that replaced Jackson's barn was located on land just to the north of the Ruthton Tribune office. It was a small, one-story wooden structure located about three blocks from Jackson's property. The plan to move it was fairly straightforward: jack it up, place wooden skids under it, attach the skids by chain to a tractor, and drag it down the street to its new location. As I recall, that plan was devised and implemented by one of David's many mentors, Clifford Rupp. This was an undertaking I absolutely had to witness, but it was scheduled for Sunday morning when I was supposed to be attending church. After some pleading, my parents agreed that I would be allowed to skip church service that one time. As a result I was a happy witness to the flawless execution of the plan, and beginning that week David and I and our pals began remodeling the new "mini-barn."

Clarence Jensen bought the Gamble Store in 1941 and remained the owner and manager until he sold it in 1972. During those decades he ranked as one of the most prominent and successful of the town's businessmen. He was admired not only for his business sense but also for having survived a polio affliction when he was young that left him paralyzed in both legs and totally dependent on crutches for mobility. He, his wife, and children lived in the apartment above the store, so he was compelled to endure the daily struggle up and down those steep, wooden, outdoor stairs on crutches. Observing that struggle was piercing to the soul. He proved to be an excellent mentor to David and came to rely heavily on him. It was Clarence who spearheaded the fund-raiser to replace the tools David lost in the fire. In some important ways Clarence Jensen represented the village of Ruthton in its role of escorting David through adolescence to adulthood.

The most challenging work I engaged in during my years in Ruthton was at the apiary during the four summers of my college years. Walter Orange, his wife Jessie, and their son Eldon were owners of the apiary which had its origins in the mid-1920s. Like many farmers who prized a high degree of self-sufficiency, they kept a few beehives on their property, and over time they added hives to their bee yard until by 1939 they had enough hives to complete the transition from farming to becoming full-time beekeepers. Their timing was excellent because war-time sugar rationing made honey a valuable commodity. The ten years between the end of the war and 1955 when I began working for them was a time of expansion in the number of hives, construction of facilities, and improvements— through trial and error—in their knowledge of the complex art of beekeeping. By 1955 they owned hundreds of beehives. Like farm-ing, beekeeping is extremely dependent on the weather, and their business was blessed that summer with perfect conditions for honey production. It led to the most productive year they had ever enjoyed. Four of us worked full time, six days a week, ten hours a day, and Walt and Eldon sometimes put in extra hours on Sundays. As we worked through that summer it gradually became apparent that if we could maintain our pace the year's harvest would guarantee the future of an enterprise the Orange family had created from scratch. It was a great privilege to be a part of that struggle and to witness their growing sense of achievement as we approached the end of a remarkable summer of honey production.

By early fall Walt and Jessie made an uncommonly bold, non-verbal announcement to the town. They traded in their old Plymouth for a Cadillac. Oddly enough, that purchase seemed to generate no resentment in a town with no luxury vehicles and a strong emphasis on thrift and humility. Even our well-off physician, Dr. Sether, abstained from such ostentation—he drove a Buick. Also, there were probably a dozen households in which poverty precluded car ownership, and yet no one seemed to begrudge the purchase of that shiny, showy Cadillac. Perhaps the explanation lay in the fact that the Oranges were hard working, they labored into old age, they had provided employment to many residents, and they together with their children and grandchildren were well regarded. Another factor favoring them was the genuine affection and respect people felt toward Jessie who always seemed to carry herself with dignity. She was born and educated in Missouri and she had a soft, lilting accent that most people found charming, almost poetic. It offered a contrast to our local speech with its strong Scandinavian and Germanic influences. By the end of 1955's honey production, Walt was entering old age, but he had arrived at his goal. The town seemed to share his delight as he and Jessie drove their Cadillac uptown on Saturday nights and parked it in a conspicuous spot on the main business street.

In contrast were Jess and Emma Larsen who owned a farm which Jess had either inherited or purchased from his father—Jess strongly asserted it was the latter. They retired in their forties—purportedly because of health considerations—moved into town close to our house, and every two or three years bought the largest available model of a new Chrysler. For those purchases they encountered barely disguised resentment. The reality that the Larsens were friendly, supportive neighbors did little to mitigate the town's negative feelings which stemmed from several factors: they were a childless couple, they had retired uncommonly early, they had not struggled financially as had so many others, they were active busy-bodies, and they were the town's exemplars of frugality. For example, when a product was advertised for sale at a discount in Pipestone's newly-opened supermarket, they hurriedly drove the thirty-five mile round trip to make the purchase, bought up to the limit allowed, and added it to the ample stores in their basement. Also, when a storm passed through the area knocking apples off their trees, they quickly gathered them up and spent days processing them into applesauce, apple butter, apple pies, apple cobbler, and apple crisp. Though they generously shared these goodies whenever they entertained, it seemed not to matter. In fact, following a wind storm other families with apple trees often invited friends and neighbors to come over with a pail and help themselves to the apples scattered on the ground.

Attitudes toward the Larsens were symbolic of some unpleasant realities of life in Ruthton. Neighborliness and good deeds did not trump long-standing resentments. Negative comments about Jess often ended with, "Wouldn't you know, just like his father, Fred

Larsen." Much of their financial success came from hard work, but jealousy deprived them of credit for it. The focus was on their presumed inherited wealth, luck, and frugality—not frugality compelled by circumstances, but a consciously-chosen frugal lifestyle which, in fairness, may have been deepened by survival lessons from the Great Depression. The noted exception to that lifestyle was those unseemly new Chryslers!

Beyond Nostalgia

Most recollections of growing up in Ruthton are pleasant, even joyful, but some are sad and contain a biting pain even unto today. One such memory from my elementary school days is of Beulah Nelson, a girl from the country who attended the Methodist Church with her two younger sisters and parents. She was one year older than I and was very bright, soft-spoken, and quite overweight. My most vivid recollection concerning her is of a Sunday evening church event concluding with adjournment to the basement for coffee and cookies while about twelve of us kids played a game of tag outside. The game quickly degenerated into a common effort to tag Beulah as often as possible to make her run and then laugh at her futile efforts to catch anyone. She gamely did her best, but her face expressed a tortured anguish followed by quiet tears which the veil cast by mid-summer's long twilight could not conceal. At that time Beulah and her sisters were attending a small country school, an intimate setting where the teacher could closely monitor student conduct. Within two or three years school consolidation forced the girls into Ruthton's school, and during that first year I heard her speak in endearing terms of her years in the country school. By her senior year when we were in the same chemistry class she seemed confident and fully able to defend herself. Whether or not she would have attended or enjoyed any of the subsequent class reunions is unknown because she passed away at an early age.

For some of Ruthton's residents the most important feature of life was a debilitating, grinding poverty that was deepest during the depression years but that persisted only to a lesser degree into the following two decades. Many families with two, three, or more children struggled to survive on the earnings of one breadwinner who worked six days a week, eight to ten hours a day in low-paying jobs of the following kind: auto or farm-implement mechanic, restaurant cook, drayman, welder, plumber's assistant, gas-station attendant, and assistant in Bill Popp's Produce and Hatchery. Many of those workers did not own a car—those who did seldom drove it—and they spent much of their limited free time at home. They infrequently went out to the movies, the bowling alley, or the local restaurants. A couple of beers seemed an extravagance. Most of these "working poor" quietly endured, but there were breakdowns, and the damage was visited onto the next generation.

An unusual case of apparent disenchantment that involves no evidence of poverty, hardship, or anger concerns a family highly esteemed in the community and good friends with my family. Bob and Ina Phillips owned a small farm on the western edge of town—it was their land that abutted the rez. Bob began working as the Great Northern Railroad agent and manager of the depot in the early 1920s, and he continued in that position until retiring about 1962. He was a serious and competent depot manager; at least he made certain that when groups of us boys hung out in the vicinity of the depot and on the tracks we never came close to attempting to climb the depot water tower, one of our long-cherished ambitions. My parents socialized regularly with Bob and Ina. They shared memberships in the PTA and Eastern Star, while Bob and Dad were fellow Masonic Lodge members. All four enjoyed mutual respect and the pleasure of each other's company.

Like many prudent depression-era families Bob and Ina had only one child, Robert—better known as "Bobby"—who was two years older than I and was one of my predecessors as stock clerk in Johnson's Store. We were friends and both of us were members of the school band as well as the town band which often gave summer concerts in the park. Bobby was very out-going and popular, had a great sense of humor, and served as Student Council President for at least one year. He was class valedictorian and he pursued a variety of interests. One evening when Don and I were at his house he showed us the short-wave radio he had assembled, and he demonstrated his ability to pick up Radio Moscow. By the time Bobby graduated from high school everyone in town knew about him. We learned even more when he began attending Augustana College in Sioux Falls where he found a part-time job as a disc jockey at a local radio station. Ruthton's residents were proud to be able to pick him up on that station sometimes in the afternoons.

One reason for the popularity of Bobby's father, Bob senior, was his gift as a speaker for special occasions such as twenty-fifth and fiftieth-wedding anniversary celebrations. I heard him several times when accompanying my parents to such events, and I, like the other attendees, enjoyed his sense of humor and his relaxed delivery of comments directed to and about the honored guests. I made an interesting discovery when I was about eight years old while attending such an event held in the basement of the Norwegian Lutheran

Church, Bob and Ina's church. When the formal program ended and everyone was getting in line for coffee, punch, cake, and cookies, I walked by where Bob had been seated and spotted a small, palm-sized piece of paper containing a series of words which turned out to be an outline of his remarks. How clever, I thought. No wonder it all seemed to flow so naturally. But, I wondered, "Is that cheating?"

Because of his skill as a speaker, his likeability, and his great sense of humor he was frequently called upon as a speaker. I recall Mom commenting more than once that Ina was always nervous while her husband spoke because she feared that in his remarks he would wander into territory that a faithful Norwegian Lutheran would find unsettling, especially in the church basement. But as the years passed it seemed to me that his commentary achieved a degree of liberation. In reality this perception may have come from the fact that I was beginning to catch the punch lines, or perhaps cultural rigidities were easing. But it is worth noting that this growing freedom of expression coincided with a marked decline in Ina's hearing!

Upon retiring and selling their farm in 1962, Bob and Ina bought an RV and hit the road. They returned to Ruthton rarely and then only for very short visits. My parents as well as others in the community were disappointed that after so many years of enjoying high esteem, long-term friendships, and a major role in the life of the town they could have so easily severed those ties. In retrospect, they may have found the separation painful, but the pain did not show. Their son Bobby likewise seemed to disappear. After college he returned to town infrequently and only for brief visits, and to the best of my knowledge he never joined us for a class reunion.

James W. Park

Aging with Class and Dignity

In recent years I have sometimes looked back to my life in Ruthton in search of examples of men who could serve as role models for aging with class and dignity. In other words, who were the respected old-timers who made it into old age with sufficient energy to maintain their interests, friendships, and joy in living. The question has come to mind recently while writing these recollections as, not coincidentally, I approach my eightieth birthday. Many of the men mentioned herein were potential candidates until they advanced closer and closer to old age and then succumbed to health problems such as arthritis, diabetes, or senility, whereupon they faded away. Others became what we referred to as "old grumps." Some of the possible role models cannot be judged because they moved away from Ruthton upon retirement, as in the case of Bob Phillips; or their departure came shortly prior to retirement, as in the case of Harry Madsen. Another likely nominee, Walter Orange, passed away at about the time of his retirement or shortly thereafter. For other possibilities I cannot bear witness because after 1960 I did not have frequent or regular contact with the community.

State Senator Hans C. Pedersen

Perhaps the most obvious candidate is the town's most prominent and prestigious man of the period; that would be Hans Pedersen, founder and president of the Farmers' and Merchants' State Bank of Ruthton, better known as Hans's Bank. This institution survived the Great Depression intact—unlike many banks of comparable size—and it continued to thrive and provide steady employment for many. Hans burnished his status by repeatedly winning election to the state senate representing southwestern Minnesota. His winning smile, polish, and charm together with certain idiosyncrasies helped him maintain popular appeal. He was noted for an uncommon fascination with the West and Southwest where he traveled frequently and on occasion prospected for gold and uranium. The lobby of his bank was graced with a large potted yucca plant and stuffed animals representative of the West such as coyote and bobcat. He was an avid hunter and was usually successful in getting a deer in the fall; in fact on a couple of occasions he traded his deer with Chris Andersen when Chris failed to get a deer but instead shot a coyote or a bobcat. Each party to those trades was happy—Chris got the deer he needed for the venison and Hans stuffed, mounted, and displayed the two varmints. Hans was also noted for a life-long habit of never tying his shoe laces except for that one time in the early 1950s while on a trip to Europe when he had a well-publicized audience with the King of Denmark. Alas, despite great qualifications, Hans fails the test because he passed away while in Arizona in search of the Lost Dutchman Gold Mine in 1959 at the age of 63—not even on the cusp of old age.

The best choice, obvious upon reviewing the past, is my grandfather, Peter Christensen. He and my grandmother lived in our house in their own upstairs apartment from 1939 until their deaths—his in 1961 and hers three years later. Our extended family was very close. We had Sunday suppers together every week, celebrated birthdays and holidays together, and shared celebrations in our respective churches. We got to know each other well during those twenty years.

My father's parents, William C. Park and Clara Shaffer Park, passed away a few years before I was born, but even though I did not know them I learned that they had a few things in common with my maternal grandparents. Both sets of grandparents were ambitious and hard working, were prominent in the community and in their respective churches, had large families, and made sacrifices so their children could be educated. And both went bankrupt and lost their farms during the depression. From conversations within the family I have surmised that my father's parents felt painfully humiliated by their misfortune, and despite their deep roots in the community they did not long delay a permanent move to California where three of their daughters lived. Like any town of its size, Ruthton offered no place to hide from such a public failure. Grandpa Park obtained work on a dairy farm in the area around Stockton, and within a few years both of the Park grandparents passed away.

In contrast, my maternal grandparents proved remarkably resilient despite severe economic challenges and the survival of only six of their eleven children into adulthood. They were a happy couple thankful for the lives they led; they remained well integrated into the community and its activities, and they were highly regarded by everyone. Grandpa kept up on current events by listening to radio newscasts every evening. He was among the crowd of local citizens who greeted President Harry Truman when his motorcade made a brief stop on main street during his 1948 campaign. Grandpa was also quite proud of having voted twice—1896 and 1908—for the Democratic presidential candidate, William Jennings Bryan, who was the voice of agrarian interests in the Midwest. An example of my grandfather's joyful outlook and love of teasing occurred whenever my dad, my brother, and I returned from our fishing excursions. But, absent an afternoon of good fishing, I did not look forward to seeing him sitting on the back steps waiting for our return so he could tease us about all the fish we had left behind. It became a summer ritual—his happy greeting, cheerful desire to see all our fish, eager examination of our empty buckets, and feigned surprise at our frequent bad luck. On occasion we had great luck, but those days were outnumbered by the "got skunked" days. So our silent prayer when setting off on our small fishing expeditions was: "Oh please, merciful

Christensen Grandparents, Golden Wedding Anniversary, 1946

goddess of fishing, bring us lots of fish or at least inspire Grandpa to take an early walk uptown before our return." But his joyful manner was such that it never produced anger or resentment.

When I was very young I remember walking hand in hand with him uptown and once in a while meeting by chance K. P. Christensen who was also an elderly Dane retired from farming and possessing a robust sense of humor. He was known as K. P. and my grandfather as Pete. The first speaker always said, "Good morning, Peter Christensen," and the second always responded, "Good morning, Peter Christensen." And then both broke out in hearty laughter over their cleverness and joy of life. Grandpa and I then continued to our destination, usually the Ruthton Co-op Creamery on the north edge of town. The creamery was a large, two-story, handsome brick building constructed in 1923 to provide a modern and enlarged outlet for the sale of milk and cream by the many farmers who kept a few milk cows as well as those with large dairy herds. The cooperative movement of local farmers had existed for more than two decades prior to that year, but its growing membership required this expanded facility. By 1940 the creamery co-op's membership exceeded 200. The butter that came from the processed milk was of a high quality as evidenced by the awards the co-op frequently received in state-wide competitions. What a treat it was to stand there with my grandfather amidst the hubbub of workers as they unloaded the fresh milk delivered by the farmers and emptied it into large vats; at the same time I tried to keep an eye on the huge horizontal churn as it slowly rotated—all the while listening to Grandpa's explanation of what I was observing. That pleasant walk to the creamery every week or so to buy a couple pounds of butter represented our modest but happy support for the frequent baking and the quality dining that took place in our home.

An opportunity for Grandpa to show his spirit came in the early 1950s in a bizarre contest of wills with the town barber, a recent arrival replacing the retired barber. The new arrival was obviously unhappy with his profession, was rather cantankerous, and occasionally forced you to wait your turn in the barber's chair located in a section of the pool hall while he finished his card game. After a year or so he announced that Saturdays were reserved for farmers, thus excluding townsmen such as my grandfather and his friends in town. The barber's new rule may have been reasonable, but certainly not in the eyes of individualists with time on their hands, time not only for haircuts at any hour or any day, but also for taking action against what they regarded as a discriminatory edict. My grandfather was a key player in a group of six or so men—fellow retirees—who organized a boycott and resistance, first by hiring a friendly barber from out of town to set up a chair in Alfred Andersen's Hardware Store one morning a month, and supplementing that with a carpool of the same men who traveled to a nearby town for their haircuts. When they returned to town they paraded through the pool hall past the barber's corner while doffing their hats! Within a few months the barber chose a different profession in a different town.

Grandpa Christensen enjoyed excellent health until diagnosed with bone cancer a few months before his death at the age of 90. Like many of his contemporaries his vision was not so good—just good enough for playing cards in good light. He owned a pair of glasses but declined to wear them. I believe Grandma had bought them for him one day at J. C. Penney on a shopping trip to Pipestone—a fairly common source for eyeglasses during the depression years. His remaining teeth had been pulled long before my time, and as a kid I assumed his false teeth were real. Aunt Bernice told the story of the day she accompanied him to the dentist for the final extractions.

Driving back to the farm in his Model A Ford he would occasionally lean out the car window to spit blood, and the car obediently followed his leftward lean into the shallow ditch; he then maneuvered it back onto the gravel road only to repeat the adventure a couple of miles farther along. For decades he wore a simple copper bracelet fashioned by his friend, Alfred Andersen, claiming it warded off arthritis. Whether it was that bracelet, his genes, or a healthy life style, he remained physically fit well into old age. He was not broken in body or spirit by a life of farm labor, walked many blocks daily, and maintained a good diet despite enjoying a variety of homemade cookies with every meal including his early breakfast. But he adhered to his motto: "Always leave the table hungry." He enjoyed his pipe despite Grandma's frequent complaints about the mess of spilled tobacco, but he did not inhale. In his late 70s he was fit enough to accept immediately a challenge from my brother and me to follow our example and climb to the top of our front-yard flagpole—about 20 feet. He did it with ease to our great surprise. Despite a life marked by serious challenges and major disappointments, his spirit was unbroken and he found great joy in life. I lovingly think of Grandpa Christensen as a worthy model for purposeful, pleasant aging.

Postscript

Since my 1954 graduation I have visited Ruthton periodically, mainly for class reunions and family visits, so I have been able to observe changes in the town, not sudden or even dramatic perhaps, but worthy of comment. Aside from the obvious changes resulting from the loss of about half of the population, closure of most of the businesses and two of the three churches, there is a general emptiness in the town emphasized by the seeming scarcity of young people. This decline is symbolized by a shift several years ago in the routing of state highway 23 which formerly ran through what was nearly the center of town bringing cars, trucks, tankers, buses, and tractors. The highway's current route truly marginalizes the town by skirting along its eastern edge so it can now quickly be bypassed with no need to slow down. Ruthton, like other small, rural communities, has been compelled to adapt to the decline in school population by consolidating its public school with those in neighboring towns. For Ruthton it has meant cooperating with Russell and Tyler so that Ruthton has grades K-5, Russell has 6-8, and Tyler has 9-12. That difficult process was accomplished in the 1980s. The loss of those upper-level grades has meant that Ruthton no longer enjoys the many athletic and music programs associated with those grades. Also missing are the many high school-related events that gave a spark to the town's social life during the school year such as freshman initiation, the junior-class play, the junior-senior banquet, school dances, homecoming, the prom, and graduation.

Ruthton's marked population decline is partly a consequence of the growing ease of movement between small towns and cities. But fundamentally it stems from the great increase in agricultural productivity over the decades and thus the shrinking need for farm labor. Driving through the countryside around Ruthton today, the reality of the depopulation of this agricultural region is noteworthy. Instead of finding two or three farms per section of land as there were fifty years ago, today there may be only one farm for every two, three, or more sections. In essence this change in the landscape shows a transition in land ownership from families to corporate entities. Dairy farms in the area have undergone a similar consolidation whereby dairymen manage herds of milk cows numbering in the hundreds. This consolidation is one of the factors contributing to a remarkable increase in agricultural productivity. Another is the introduction of ever larger and more efficient farm machinery and improved technology in the application of fertilizer, herbicides, and pesticides. For example, instead of planting four rows of corn at a time, the larger equipment allows the planting of twenty-four or more rows. Instead of controlling weeds by periodic cultivation, that vital function is now done by applying herbicides. A focus on growing only one or two crops, corn and soybeans, has also improved productivity as has the introduction of new and greater-yielding hybrids.

To accommodate the consequent growth in output, Ruthton has witnessed in recent times the construction of a large grain elevator together with additional silos and cement bunkers—all for storage of beans and corn while awaiting shipment by rail. A mile-long railroad side track that can handle a freight train of up to 110 cars has also been added; it can be fully loaded in sixteen hours. The corporation that owns these storage facilities, Cenex Harvest States Cooperatives, has also added a fertilizer plant for the processing, sale, and distribution of its product in the surrounding region. To further accommodate the region's vast output of corn, three large ethanol-processing facilities have been built within forty miles of Ruthton—to the north in Marshall, to the south in Luverne, and to the west in Aurora, South Dakota. An additional example of dynamic change can be witnessed in a glance to the west of town along Buffalo Ridge or to the hills south of town where those modest heights are dotted with scores of huge windmills for generating electrical power. To these physical signs of progress can be added what may be seen as a sign of an inner vitality: construction in recent times of a community church on the outskirts of town.

These are the mixed forces propelling the marked increase in agricultural productivity, the hollowing out of small agricultural towns, and the alteration in lasting, fundamental ways of life across small-town America. But the passing of that era of the mid-twentieth century should not be mourned. It was a time of heavy labor and long workdays that often produced no more than a marginal existence. It does seem, however, that growing up at that time helped instill positive values. Most striking was an unquestioned optimism about our nation's future. That optimism was born of an unquestioned pride in our nation's history and accomplishments and of a clear sense of the growing ability of the United States to shape the course of world history at a time of genuine challenge. Surviving the Great Depression and emerging victorious from World War II contributed to this palpable confidence in our values and to a certainty of purpose. The erosion in recent times of such a positive outlook partly explains the nostalgic appeal of those mid-twentieth century decades in rural Minnesota. I am not alone in feeling a warm nostalgia and also a sense of gratitude to the village of Ruthton for the memories of the way it was and for its role in shaping our values and getting us started.

CPSIA information can be obtained
at www.ICGtesting.com
Printed in the USA
BVHW02*0730260718
522653BV00005B/6/P